A MASTER MARINER'S TALE

A MASTER MARINER'S TALE

DAVID STEVENSON

CAEDMON OF WHITBY

ISBN 0 905355 55 5

First published in 2002 by
Caedmon of Whitby
Headlands
128 Upgang Lane
Whitby
North Yorkshire
YO21 3JJ

Printed and bound by
SMITH SETTLE
Ilkley Road, Otley, West Yorkshire LS21 3JP

For Joyce and Hilary
who have always come with me on my travels

ACKNOWLEDGEMENTS

I have to thank Tom Binks for giving permission to include his accounts of Whitby which appear in the appendices. I am grateful to Ernest Butler for his continued encouragement, and to Ann Livsey for her invaluable help and most practical assistance in deciphering my hand writing for her excellent work on the typescript.

The pictures have come from many sources, not least from my colleagues, Hugh Edwards in Jeddah and Angus McDonald in Takoradi; from John Scott, a Tyne ferry veteran; from Irene Ellis and Sheila Linney who both had vivid memories of ferry days. The cameo on the title page is by courtesy of Captain P. Adams of the Honourable Company of Master Mariners.

CONTENTS

CHAPTER ONE
OIL FOR THE LAMPS OF ARABIA

'That's what you want,' said John Nash as we stood yarning while we waited for the pilot in Heysham Lake to berth us on the oilberth. It was 5 am and a smart little ship, the *Duke of Rothesay* sailed past us. 'My brother-in-law is second officer on that one. He'll be home on his bike by six o'clock, have breakfast and into bed. He sails tonight at midnight into Belfast by 7.30 am.'

It was a long time before I was to turn this dream into reality. Readers of *Ship and Shore* will recall that when I decided to leave the oil tanker world the first ship I then joined was the *Suilven*, a converted private yacht which was to be a pilot cutter in the Persian Gulf. After which I worked on the Shatt al Arab, down the Gulf on port and sea towage from Abadan between Bushire, Kuwait, Bahrein and Bandar Abbas, towing six-hundred ton barges loaded with case oil (*ie* Kerosene oil) for heating and lighting. I was Mate on the Sea Tug *Zurmand*, a 1,000 hp tug with Captain Robertson. When we went down to Rooka Channel to tow a grounded tanker off, we always went with Bill Scource on the ST *Bahramand*. In the common fog patches, Bill always took the lead, shouting to us as he passed, 'Follow Father, he'll get you there!'

In my first week *Zurmand* was sent down the gulf to recover a fairway buoy adrift from Bandar Mashur channel. It was a rough northerly wind and once we had found the buoy, located after receiving radio messages from passing ships, we took it in tow and headed into northerly rough seas, into which the bows of the tug dipped frequently. The sea found its way down the anchor spurling pipes into the chain locker and forehold. To get into the forehold one had to lift a deck hatch over which lived twenty-six Indian crew members. As I approached the hatchway almost all of them were seasick amid groans, retches and moans. Somehow I held my stomach together, with great effort, and called to serang (bosun) and those who were able to follow me into the hold with our electric torches where we found water to the depth of two feet; it sloshed and rushed from side to side, drenching our stores of six months with which we were supplied.

'Get to the strum boxes,' I ordered and we worked in the foetid air to shift sufficient stores to reveal the boxes fitted over the pump drain lines. Both were choked with cotton waste, paper and heaven knows what else.

My old friend the Suilven *was now converted into the pilot cutter* Shahnaz.

In moments, word came from the engine room that the bilge water was now coming freely from forehold suctions and over the side.

• • •   • • •   • • •

The fire duty tug was *Lady Curzon*, a twin-screw steam vessel of 800 hp. In daylight she was used as a bow tug to help 'turn off' the tankers on all twenty-two berths. At sunset she went down to number 9 buoy right opposite the spirit jetties and was moored only by a slip wire.

Before I went to bed Jimmy and I had a smoke and a yarn. The Shatt Al Arab river looked so lovely and peaceful under the lights of Abadan refinery. Just as I turned in I heard a soft explosion and my duty watchman, Sukkuni Abdul Ahab was at my cabin door.

'Sahib, Sahib,' he shouted. 'Big ship go boom.' As I opened my door the river seemed aflame. I got the crew on standby and told Jimmy Rigden, the chief engineer to get all our fire pumps going on the after deck. I started to blow the fire alarm whistle – six shorts and one long – regularly. This would alert the other twelve tugs in port.

I came downstream on the far side until I could swing across towards no 20 Jetty and the flaming torch which was MV *Aurelian*, a 15,000 ton Norwegian

2

tanker of almost new proportions. The wind was blowing from bow to stern and all of the bridge structure was one great bonfire. But also on her main deck towards her after parts scattered pools of petrol made a series of fires. I handled *Lady Curzon* from forward of bridge alongside to the poop. My Iranian crew were terrified but were willing to do as the ship and myself directed. Immediately in front of the bridge stood a tower of two monitors, and one fore and aft of her funnel, operated manually. Manoeuvring hard alongside, I moved the tug from before the bridge, right aft to the poop deck and used the monitors to douse and sweep over the flames of the tanker from portside to overside on starboard. As I was doing this the Firemaster of the river came on board from launch number one.

By this time the shore fire brigade was pumping foam into the lower part of the bridge. 'Good work,' he shouted over the roar of fire and rush of water, 'use your monitors to drench the top bridge.' So I moored bow on just before the front of the bridge and allowed the monitors a maximum elevation to let the breeze break the jets into a severe rain-like shower to douse the top flames, assisted by the monitors of six more tugs who had come alongside to help. Once, as I had run from poop to bridge, the petrol tank of the port bridge lifeboat exploded, to shower the after deck of *Lady Curzon* with flaming petrol to set the very tug on fire. But it was short lived due to Jimmy directing the staring eyed crew to use hand fire extinguishers to effect.

It took the shore fire brigade and our seven tugs from just after midnight to 11 am next day to leave *Aurelian*, still smouldering, and shifted from the now ruined 22 jetty to the buoys mid river.

The reason for the fire was found to be that when the petrol cargo flexibles were opened, the receiving tank valves on the ship were closed and a flexible hose burst and flaying about struck a jetty lamp, fractured it, and the spark ignited a great jet of flaming petrol over the bridge house. The officers and men in the bridge accommodation all escaped by dashing forward to the bow and made pier head jumps, some fifty feet into the flow of the river, to be rescued by the fire launch.

◆ ◆ ◆   ◆ ◆ ◆   ◆ ◆ ◆

Once we helped in laying an underwater ten-inch pipeline at Umm Said south of Bahrain. The tanker *British Drummer* had a large towage winch to assist any of the Company's ships between the Gulf and the UK. With two anchors spread ahead of her, her ten-inch towing wire was led ashore and secured to the end of the pipeline which lay back into the desert on rollers. *Zurmand* and *Zerang* made fast on either shoulder of *British Drummer* and when all was ready (no radio was used at that time) *Drummer* blew three long blasts and it all began. She hove on both anchors, and went 'full ahead' while we tugs did the same, keeping our eyes on transit marks back on shore, as the hose moved into the sea the rollers fell off into a large pit dug into the beach with the labourers leaping clear and yelling. And we succeeded in one long haul of some 1.500 feet which would serve small ships in the future.

The tug skipper of the *Herald* and I acquired a twelve foot motor boat which had been a trawler lifeboat. We would take our wives, daughters and dog for picnics up the inside of Boat Club Island, then round into the main river and

The old lifeboat was converted for our own use and our dog, Polly, approved of it.

Piloting a ship meant more than simply standing on the bridge.

back to the club. Good fun. One day in July Peter and I took the boat for a run to check the motor which had not been running well. We went up Boat Creek with daughters and dog and stopped at the entrance to the river for a spell, then decided to go back to the club the long way, right round the Boat Island. It was 120°F and on the river the heat was tremendous. We had just got into the main river when we ran out of petrol. Imagine two professional sailors being so stupid. We didn't even have one oar with which we could have sculled back safely. We were able to give the little girls our one orange and the dog a pannier of oily tasting river water while Peter and I suffered the dreadful thirst.

Just as we thought there was no one on the river, from out of the reed beds came an Iraqi man in a home made canoe made out of a forty gallon oil drum, cut in half, riveted together and shaped double ended, in which the Arab was paddling. When we hailed him he came over and when we said 'Boat Club', he smiled and towed us to the Iraqi bank, where a handful of local planters greeted us. To thank the Arab boatman we gave him our cigarettes and he left with a big smile. Peter and I pointed to the petrol tank and held up an empty oil canister. One man grabbed it and disappeared into the Palm trees. 'We've lost that' I said when just then another man appeared. He greeted us with 'Salaam alikum' and pointed to each of us said 'You Captain sahib *Herald*', and to me he said 'You Captain *Zurmand* tug'. We smiled and waited only a few more moments when back came the canister full of petrol. Before we left we discovered that our friend was coxswain of one of our motor launches *Hamamet,* and so a few days later he called at the tug moorings where we rewarded him with a carton of cigarettes.

The steam tug Zurmand.

6

Abadan Boat Club, the Barge.

Another time I took the motor boat on my own to call a mile downstream to the Dredger *Haffar*, and collected a carton of beer. It was a rather foolish thing to do as it was nearly sunset. Half a mile from the *Haffar* the engine conked and as I was trying to steer it a canoe from the Iraqi side thumped alongside containing six river men. All of them looked threatening, one particularly wielding a knife and saying to the rest by pointing to me and the river the individual said 'over side.'

Fortunately one of the Company's fast launches was passing and I waved to him. He pulled over and recognising me he took me in tow after a few nasty words to the Iraqi canoe crowd.

I'm sure I've told you that the Shatt Al Arab river was the border between Iraq and Iran. Those of us who worked in Abadan resolved that to be moored to Abadan jetties or on a BP vessel we were not in Iraq. If we were tied to a jetty awaiting a tanker and the Iranian Coastguard who manned the jetty we had our duty *Sukunni* to shout 'Stand by' and we would let go all jetty moorings. Steer off the jetty for fifty metres, let go our anchor and haul up the courtesy flag of Iraq at the foremast and leave the fuming coast guard exchanging words with our Indian crew.

7

The last promotion I had in Abadan was to act as Chief Officer of *Haffar* a twin ladder suction dredger whose master was Ronnie Dickson who had transferred from Iraqi Port Authority's dredger fleet which kept the delta mouth of the Shatt Al Arab River dredged by keeping Rooka Channel deep enough for the scores of tankers which visited Abadan.

Haffar was to dredge the river jetties deep enough for deep drafted ships and now had her own special berth a mile downriver of the jetties. Her dredging pipes were three feet in diameter and her discharge pipe connected to a flexible one and her cargo of 1760 cubic yards discharged into a reclamation 'bund' whose purpose was to improve the flow of the river. Captain Ronnie and I had to get to the berth from our homes by taxi, then walk a quarter of a mile over the reclaimed sand where *Haffar* was moored. It was rather like walking along a damp beach. Robbie always wanted to examine the spoil discharged the previous day, and while he headed towards the mouth of the pipe I kept carefully on the drier beach. One foggy morning carrying his raincoat and brief case, he disappeared from me in the fog. All of a sudden I heard him shout 'Dave come and help.'

As I hurried over, the sand around one began to act like a quicksand, and I found myself up to the knees and sinking. I caught sight of Ronnie floundering up to the chest in a dangerous situation. I called out to him 'throw your raincoat out in front of you and climb on to it.' This he did while I walked in up to the waist beside him.

We had been calling out 'Help' hoping that the *Haffar* crew would hear us. When suddenly six Arab workers appeared with long handled spades, used to keep putting up the edge of the bund. By reaching out to us two long spades they were able to pull us to safety. When we got on board we looked at each other; Ronnie had been up to his neck in this quicksand and myself up to my waist. We had a good drink. We were able to phone from the ship to report to Marine Superintendent Captain Sinnot, ordered a taxi and when Ronnie dropped off at his home in Bawarda he said he'd call my wife up in Braim. And when I finally did get home my beloved Joyce looking at my soaking self and sniffing the powerful whisky odour as I kissed her didn't really believe my story till she called Ronnie's wife and got the whole story.

It was not very long before my two year contract ended and I wrote to British Rail before we flew off from Abadan.

CHAPTER TWO

HEYSHAM

THE MOUNTAINS OF MOURNE SWEEP DOWN TO THE SEA

I had been on a waiting list at Heysham for several years, as promotion in their fleet was in 'dead mens shoes' and could be a lengthy business. I wrote to the Irish Seas Company to say I was available for work shortly before leaving Abadan. And it was a pleasure to receive their letter offering me a post as third officer (cargo). My wife and I got settled in Heysham village in short order and I joined my first ship, the *Duke of Argyll*. Imagine my surprise and pleasure to meet, once again, my old seafaring friend, John Nash, whose words had fired me so long before.

••• ••• •••

Very soon I found myself on watch in charge of a fast 4,000 ton ferry filled with passengers and cargo. Between Belfast and Heysham are 126 miles by the course we took, and doing 18 to 20 knots the time taken was seven hours. The navigation plan, previously prepared by the chief officer and master was on the chart table to be used by the officer on watch.

Irish Sea weather can often contribute to a rough passage. My seafaring training over the years had been to 'husband' the ship, or to heave-to if the sea was coming over the bow. One particular night there was a severe northwest gale coming down Georges Channel and creating really bad weather. The course was taken up the east course of the Isle of Man, then at a certain point off Whitehaven alter course 60° to port and pass five miles off Point of Ayre till abeam four miles off Mull of Galloway.

Running up the Isle of Man gave us a bit of shelter and the sleek, greyhound shape of the *Duke of Lancaster* had a gentle roll which altered dramatically as she changed into a pitching movement, accepting the increased seas over her bow, still doing 18 knots. I watched her carefully till she dipped severely and scooped a green sea over her fore hatch and deck to thunder up against our bridge house and splash into the wheelhouse. As soon as this happened I rang 'slow ahead' to the engine room and blew down the voice pipe to the Captain, snug in his bed.

My first cross-channel ship, the second Duke of Lancaster.

With all furnaces and boiler at full pressure on both funnels the safety valves blew with a deafening roar and the engine room had me answering the phone when Captain Sergeant appeared and pushed the telegraph back to 'full speed' and calmly started to fill his pipe. 'Captain,' I said, 'she was shipping green seas over the bow and my training was always to 'husband' the ship.' 'Hrrmph' was his reply, 'I'll stop here to the Mull.' He then told me that the maximum time, Heysham to Belfast was seven hours and twenty minutes. 'If the ship is over that time,' he said, 'the master has to write a letter of explanation of the Marine Manager. 'Can I tell you,' he went on, 'I became Master of this ship in 1928 when she was launched.' He had a good puff on his pipe, flooding the wheelhouse with pungent smoke. He ended, 'And I've never had to write that letter.' He went on to tell me how seaworthy those cross-channel railway boats were. Within a couple of weeks I was used to the Irish Sea conditions, – not to mention the passengers, on average 700-900 a trip and up to 1200-1500 over Christmas and the 12th July week.

Like British Rail, we had First and Third class. First class passengers had two berth cabins and there were four staterooms up on A deck. Third class all lived in the after part of the ship on D deck, adjacent to the after hold and known as 'steerage'. It was an extra large room fitted with plywood benches all around the walls and in rows across with a sort of space in the middle, used for dancing to Irish music on occasions.

I was called once by the Petty Officer Lamptrimmer to say that some gypsy folk were cooking a meal in the steerage. When I went down I found there were two primus stoves, one boiling a kettle and the other a frying pan. I quoted the fire regulations to all and had the stoves confiscated till we reached port. Another evening we got the shout 'Man overboard!' By the time the message reached the bridge we had travelled three miles. We turned around and slowed right down where we thought the person might be. Using our searchlight and Aldis signal lamp; we found nothing and had to return to passage some fifteen minutes late. It seemed that a soldier on leave had been on the poop deck when, from out of the steerage door came a sobbing girl. She paused then stood on a mooring bollard and stepped over in front of his eyes. Of course it took him time to find a steward and all this delay meant the loss of a passenger. At Donegal Quay on our arrival four RUC officers escorted the soldier for questioning, for he could have been the means of 'helping her overboard.'

My first promotion came after a year, to Second Officer, cargo. I left the mail boats and went on *Slieve Bawn*, one of the cargo vessels based in Heysham. 1,500 tons and 15 knots speed, she too had to keep a schedule. Sail from Heysham at 2200 hr and arrive at 0800 hr the following morning, berthing one hour after our mail boat. All three cargo boats were named after the mountains of Mourne, *Slieve Bawn*, *Slieve Bearnagh* and *Slieve League*. A fourth one, *Slieve Donard* was based in Holyhead to run between Holyhead and Dublin.

The cargo officer's life was interesting, from carrying on deck the early railway containers to getting a hundred cars in the 'tween decks. Each was lifted on board in a special sling, then manhandled up each side of the hatchway, and lashed down with plump straw cushions between their bumpers.

A passenger on the mail boat from Heysham would wonder why his car was not on his ship among the four or five the mail boat could take on her hatches. He was a very surprised person who, prepared to complain to the Purser at not having his car on board, was told politely to go and have his breakfast and his car would be waiting for him in the transit shed of Donegal Quay.

Once we travelled from Portsmouth to Le Havre and all the cars in the car decks, including mine, were lying one behind the other, with no brakes on and certainly no straw padding fenders.

I remember well that one time a circus was to travel from Heysham to Belfast on *Slieve Bawn*. All the animals, including an elephant, were to be walked on board over a stout gangway. All except the elephant, who stood on the dock giving little trumpetings, putting one foot on the gangway then standing back. He was sure the gangway was not strong enough. Until one of the old dockers had a bright idea. In front of the elephant's eyes he got a few men to lay on top of the gangway six stout cattle-pen boards. Jumbo put his foot back on again, trumpeting in triumph he calmly walked into the 'tween deck' among the familiar smells of the previous cargoes of cattle, sheep and pigs.

CHAPTER THREE

FROM COLONY TO REPUBLIC. GOLDCOAST TO GHANA 1950-57

In late 1951 I travelled to Millbank to the offices of Crown Agents for the Colonies, and successfully passed the interview for an appointment as Marine Officer with Gold Coast Railways and Harbours Board in the port of Takoradi, Gold Coast. Presently I sailed from Liverpool on board 'MV *Apapa*,' one of the Elder Dempster's three fine passenger ships serving the needs of the travelling public (mostly Colonial/Government servants) to Bathurst Gambia, Freetown Sierra Leone, Takoradi Gold Coast and Lagos Nigeria. In those days the Liverpool landing stage was always full of passenger ships from all over the world. Cunard to New York and Canada, CPR to Canada with its beautiful *'Empress'* Liners, Shaw Saville & Albion to Australia and New Zealand, P & O to India and the Far East. On the Mersey itself were colliers, tramps, tugboats, tankers, and lighters, all creating a wonderful panorama of bustling, busy marine activity.

At two o'clock we were turned off the berth by two fussing tugboats and stood out bravely downriver to the bar, leaving the smoking grime of Liverpool and the Liver Building to disappear into the distance astern; two hours later we had dropped the pilot off Lynas, North Wales and we were really on our way.

The liners *Accra*, *Apapa* and *Aureol* were 14,000, ton motor ships, designed to take 350 First Class and 120 Second Class passengers. Elder Dempsters directors had first hand knowledge of the West African scene of the times, realising that those who went out there to work tended to endure rather arduous conditions, particularly if they went up country, or 'bush' as it was known. So both way out and home the voyage was made as comfortable and as luxurious as possible. Fifty years ago we were having First Class Transatlantic comfort on the West African run. Captain's cocktail party. Dressing for dinner every night. Seven course meals and waiter service individual to each table. Early morning tea in one's cabin, (en suite). At 10.30 soup or Bovril on deck, varied in the tropics to ice cream and cool drinks. Deck games. Swimming pool. Cinema. Various bars. Dancing on deck. Captain's Party. All these things, coupled with good food and company set people up for their arduous 12-18 month stint of duty in the service of Crown Agents.

One of the three Elder Dempster Mail ships in Takoradi harbour.

Amrado *at work, pushing up the bow of the* Apapa.

We sailed on 18th December 1951 and so we spent Christmas at sea, calling at Las Palmas after five days, Bathurst seven days, Freetown nine days and finally Takoradi after twelve days.

We docked at 6 am on 30th December, as the shoreline of the Gold Coast rose out of the early morning haze something impinged on my consciousness which was to remain with me all the years I spent on the Coast. Indeed I only have to close my eyes and listen and I hear it again – the deep, rolling, continuous boom of the Atlantic surf, breaking endlessly on the beaches.

Within a few days I had met the then Marine Superintendent Captain Anderson, had been introduced to my fellow Marine Officers, 4 Pilots, 3 tugmasters, and I was given training in how tug operations were done in Takoradi harbour. I was already an experienced 'tuggie' having had two years of it in Abadan, but the little local wrinkles had to be discovered, and the 'feel' of a different type of tug boat found.

Takoradi and Sekondi are/were twin towns on the Gold Coast situated 400 miles North of the Equator, right in the Bight of Benin. An old sea faring rhyme has this to say of the Bight.

> *Sailor – 'Beware of the Bight of Benin*
> *Few come out – tho many go in.'*

The Gold Coast was part of West Africa, one relatively small part of that great bulge of the African Continent which stretches from Senegal, round into the Bight of Benin and ending one could say at the Congo. Starting from Senegal and coming round the 'bulge' we have Senegal (French) Gambia (British) Guinea Bissau (French) Guinea (British) Sierra Leone (British) Liberia (US) Ivory Coast (French) Ghana (British) Togo (TVT – Trans Volta Togoland) Benin (TVT) Nigeria (British) Cameroon (German) (British) (Portuguese) Gabon (French) Congo (Belgium). To the north of these countries and extending the full width of the African continent from Mauritania to Egypt and Sudan was the vast sweep that used to be marked on the map of the world as French Equatorial Africa – now divided into many sovereign states. Mali, Niger, Chad, Central African Republic and the rest.

Roughly speaking, looking at a map Ghana's coast extends approximately 400 miles from east to west and the country reaches almost 900 miles north to the border of Upper Volta. Its eastern boundary is marked by the Volta River, and when we lived there forty-five years ago Togo was also administered by Gold Coast Government as Trans-Volta-Togoland (TVT). Later TVT became two separate small states of Togo and Benin, squeezed between Ghana and Nigeria.

The main coastal towns of the Gold Coast were Axim on the border of the Gold Coast and Takoradi/Sekondi, Cape Coast, Winneba and Accra. Accra was

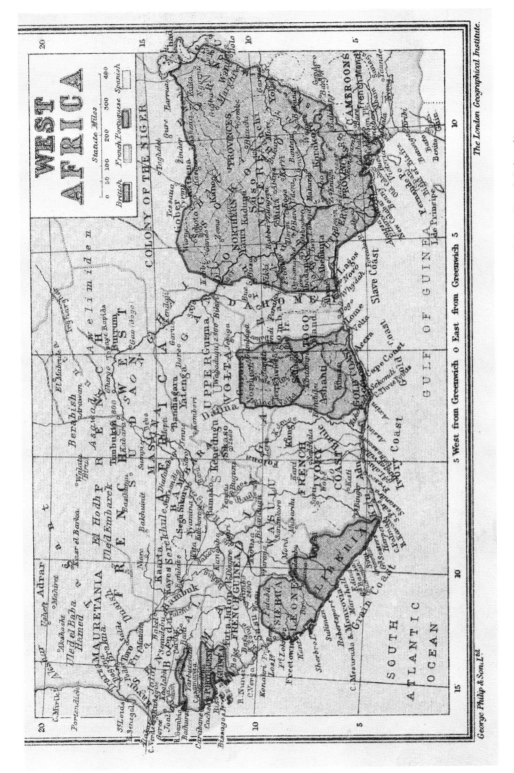

West Africa from a 1934 atlas, showing the old colonial names including Takoradi and Sekondi.

the seat of provincial government under Colonial office and was a major city of some 250,000.

Takoradi/Sekondi had a population of 37,000. The other coastal ports were what were called surf ports *ie:* they had no port facilities, only an open roadstead where ships anchored some half a mile offshore and *all* cargo had to be transferred by surf canoe, more of that later.

Around 1912 a railway line was built from Sekondi to Achimota (300 miles) and another, to meet it from Accra started and reached as far as Koforidua (200 miles). Sekondi became the main railway workshops area and locomotives and rolling stock, rails and all the stuff needed to build railways were loaded by canoes, both at Sekondi and Accra. Brunel would have been proud of our British engineering skill. The original loco landed through the surf in 1912, in pieces by canoes. This was used in the 1950s to haul the local commuter train between Takoradi and Sekondi.

After the First World War the need for a proper deep water port was vital to the Gold Coast and Takoradi was chosen. Mainly because of the way the reef ran offshore tending to protect the bay toward Sekondi. The original idea was to copy the design of Marseilles. A long curving outer breakwater, which could be extended as need and conditions allowed, with several main finger piers leading out from the shore to give berthage, warehousing and rail connection to the rest of the country.

By 1921 Takoradi Port existed. A long L shaped breakwater of 1¼ miles sheltering a main finger pier, of 4 ocean going berths, 9 Buoy berths and log pond storages for up to 8,000, hardwood logs. The main exports of the Gold Coast were cocoa, timber, manganese bauxite and palm oil. Imports were vehicles, and all types of consumer goods, transported by rail and road to all the small outlying bush stations and villages.

In every small settlement one would find for example the red and black logo of John Holt, Liverpool. This store would be managed by a Lebanese manager or latterly by an African. These little stores were stocked with enamel cooking pots, basins, trade tobacco leaf, salt, tea, various tools, hammers, axes and the cutlass or panga, a fearsome looking knife with a curved tip, made in heavy grade steel, used for chopping down trees, clearing the bush, cutting grass and around the house for chopping firewood for the wood-burning stoves then common to most houses. These pangas are universal throughout Africa and have been one of the main weapons used many years ago by the Mau Mau in Kenya, and we all remember how terrible that was, and the more recent and even more hideous slaughter of innocent thousands in Ruanda/Burundi.

I had one occasion to be thankful for a panga. My wife and daughter and I lived in a standard colonial style bungalow surrounded by garden and a drive running right around it. We were protected at night by a night watchman, thoughtfully provided by the Harbour Board. Ours was a NT Boy called Yessa who was extremely good. For some time we had been concerned about a Black Mamba which lived in the garden compost heap, but was always too quick to be attacked, sliding swiftly away at the slightest approach of a human. Yessa was determined to get this snake. I don't know how he did it but at 2 am one morning I was awakened by him tapping on the mosquito screening of the bedroom window.

'Massa – Massa – come see!' I got up and went out on to the verandah. There stood Yessa, panga in one hand dripping blood. In the other, held proudly aloft, the seven foot headless body of the Mamba, its body looking for all the world like a length of four inch braided steel wire.

Something now about how we lived in West Africa. I had to wait eight months in 1952 for my wife and child to join me. I said that most of the travel to and fro from West Africa was by sea but the airlines were beginning to make inroads into the travel business. BOAC had started to use forty-one seat Argonauts flying via Rome, Kano, Accra, Lagos and small feeder aircraft would fly Accra-Kumaasi-Takoradi.

I finally got my own bungalow in August 1952 and Joyce and Hilary (aged eighteen months) arrived by air, one exciting morning at Takoradi Airport. The plane which brought them from Accra was a DH Dove five-seater, very cramped and when the door opened on to the tarmac, the first thing which tumbled on the ground was Hilary's pottie!

But we soon settled in, though I'm sure Joyce could tell you a lot about the problems of coming to terms with the natural hazards of wildlife around the bungalow. Ants of various sizes, so persistent that all food was kept in a netted safe, standing on legs which in turn stood in empty fruit tins containing Kerosene. Malarial mosquitos were persistent, dealt with by bedroom netting and sprays and prophylactic pills – very effective most of the time. After dark, attracted by our lights and coming through the open doors and windows, were giant moths, smaller moths, praying mantis. All of which were in turn preyed on by tiny gekkos, beautiful little lizards. The worst pests of all were the cockroaches – real Bombay Canaries reaching $2\frac{1}{2}$ inches long, very fast on their feet, and I used to swear, could *think*. The most effective way to deal with them was to lay six inches from the edge of the skirting, a mixture of sugar and borax overnight. In the morning, the houseboy would sweep up scores of bodies and we would be free for a spell.

Joyce was very fond of gardening and with the household staff we had – modest by some standards – she spent a lot of time with her plants and later with her animals. Our staff consisted of a cook/steward, washboy and gardenboy. Joyce managed them all very well and they in turn seemed to like her. We never had any trouble. Or perhaps I should correct that. For several years we

Our house, a standard colonial-style bungalow.

had an excellent steward called Mensah – first rate. But he had a very handsome and flighty wife called Grace. Grace used to get all dolled up and go off to town and sort of forget to come back. I don't think she did anything really naughty, but poor old Mensah used to get very worked up.

One night we were awakened by the most enormous commotion, coming from the servants quarters, some 50 yards away in the compound. It sounded like murder was being done. I went out to see what it was all about. I found Grace, her mouth bleeding, a real virago of a woman in a fearsome temper screaming in Fanti at Mensah and a whole lot of her things out of the house in the drive; Mensah, his face a picture of misery patiently picking up each piece of goods and putting it back in the room, while she just as wildly threw it out again. Finally she attacked him but Yessa, the watchman, who had been in the police, simply threw his arms around her and held her spitting and screeching. I kept saying 'tomorrow – in the morning. Tomorrow Grace. Please!' Eventually she calmed down and went into the house and peace returned to Bedukrome Road.

There was no sign of Grace at 9 am next day, I asked Mensah what had happened. 'Massa – I tell her go to town, but make sure you come back early not late. She come back at 1 am. So – I slap um'. It was not long before Mensah gave his notice and left to follow his Grace, who had departed to Accra.

Ready for the next tour of duty.

Our daughter Hilary with Mensah.

We then got Sam, a much older boy/man. Sam was even better than Mensah. He had one fault, on Saturday afternoon he would go to Takoradi town to visit his friends, and come back to serve dinner for us at 8 pm. Only – he was almost always tipsy. Very happy but not quite up to his usual standard of service. Most Saturdays we had friends for dinner and Sam was always warned about this. It got to a stage where Joyce would fire Sam every Saturday night and every Sunday morning at 5.50 am we would be awakened by Sam, working furiously in the lounge, dining room and kitchen, polishing furniture and floors – in the hope that Madam would re-instate him.

Joyce's Pets

During our stay in the Gold Coast, my wife, who has always been fond of animals, gradually acquired a variety of pets. First off we got a small black fluffy kitten named Cleopatra, she grew into a handsome black Persian-type cat, and was with us for seven years. A little girl friend of ours, going home to England for school left us Che Che, her Putty Nosed Monkey – a small fruit and nut case if ever there was one. He was a proper Houdini. We kept him – most of the time – in a large wire net cage, which he would patiently work away at till he had made a hole big enough to escape from. We kept chickens in a hen house, but again, they always seemed to get out. Joyce did get eggs from time to time but it was by stalking the particular hen to find its 'lay' rather than out of the coop. We even had a Gazelle for several months. Someone donated it to us again on their passage through Takoradi. I had to be very firm and say NO, when she got the offer of the most gorgeous baby chimp, "only £14 Massa!" I've always found it difficult to resist anything my wife wants but this – well – NO. The best pet we had was Jacko a West African Grey Parrot. We got him in 1953 when he had been captured along with a lot of young birds, somewhere up north, and brought down by traders to be sold in the markets and around the bungalows. Hilary then 2½ got to choose him from two, – naturally she chose the bigger bird, the other – much younger went to our dear friend Dorothy. Jacko, for so he was called, had been badly treated, and was a very frightened bird. A frightened parrot is a fierce parrot. All he had was a big beak. But boy could he use it. He also had a screech, a raucous, continuous noise which started as soon as a human approached his cage. I kept saying to my wife 'let's get rid of him. Swop for a younger quieter bird. You'll never tame him'. To which Joyce simply said 'you have patience dear, just wait and see'. Each day she would go round the corner of the verandah to where the cage held Jacko and just talk to him. At first from a distance. But gradually getting nearer. He stopped squawking and began to listen. I just left it to her till one day, some three months later she called me to come and watch quietly. When I turned the corner, I could scarcely believe my eyes. Her fingers were inside the bars and she was stroking the parrots head, while he kept up a low happy chuckle noise. It was a miracle.

Eventually Jacko got the run of the bungalow, bossing the cat and my daughter, and talking – yes talking. We all know you ladies can talk, and I can only tell you that our polly was famous in Takoradi among the local servants as 'dat polly fit talk jus like Madam!'

'Good morning. Goodnight. Hellooo!! Ha Ha Ha Ha.' (This was in my voice.) 'Mensah pass coffee'.

When we left Africa for good we brought him home on the 'Aureol' to Liverpool and he spent the night in the Adelphi Hotel reception desk. When we came down to breakfast, he had the guests and staff in kinks as he chatted away to them.

We lived in Belfast at that time and I had to cross Liverpool/Belfast on the ferry. Where alas due to National Health Regulations he had to go into one months quarantine in Bellevue Zoo – where we used to visit him each weekend. He lived with us for seventeen years until he fell off his perch one teatime and was dead as he hit the bottom of the cage.

R I P Jacko.

CHAPTER 4
COCOA & LOCOS

Respect the right of all peoples to choose the form of government under which they will live.

Let me turn again to how the trade of Gold Coast was carried on. I have said that cocoa was a main export. Grown up country on farms. The cocoa bush is a small tree about 8-10 feet tall, and producing under cultivation large oval pods about the size of an Ostrich egg. Inside this pod are the beans, dark red, about twice the size of a broad bean. These are husked, the beans, sun dried are packed into 1 cwt gunny bags, and shipped by road/rail to the coastal ports. The main company involved in our day, was Cadbury/Fry working with the shipping companies of Palm Line, Elder Dempster, John Holts, Barber Line, Woermann Line and Holland West Africa Line, all using ships of around 10,000, tons on 24 feet draft 460 feet length, ocean going and also able to traverse the rivers and creeks of Nigeria and Congo.

Let us use Accra as an example.

When the cocoa season was in full swing thousands of tons of cocoa would be landed down to the beach a mile west of the city. A short breakwater only half a mile long protected the beach from the main force of the thundering surf, yet the 200 surf canoes had the arduous task of working out through the surf to the ships, work alongside, then return again through the surf and land on the beach, to pick up a sling of 25 sacks of cocoa. Each canoe, made of mahogany, measured twenty-four feet, double ended and was propelled by 8 paddlers and a steersman. All were highly skilled, from the Kroo tribe mostly, from the Ivory Coast, employed on a contract by Elder Dempster and Palm Line.

The beach loading operations were master-minded by young ex-seagoing staff from the companies, who hoped to move upwards in the firm. Their task was to co-ordinate the loading gangs from the warehouses, down to the beach marshall to collect the bags as they were loaded on to the canoes. Imagine a wide bay with a dozen big cargo ships lying fairly close together, anchored about half a mile off the beach, rolling under a hot blue sky. Between them and the shore, scores of big surf canoes are plying either outwards or inwards, light or loaded. Alongside each ship are a dozen canoes, several at each cargo hatch, clamouring to be unloaded.

Liparus *being berthed – Cargo of asphalt.*

At the beach would be at least 12 canoes heading at breakneck speed through the surf, riding it like a roller coaster, to land with a grinding crunch on the sands, while all eight boys leapt out laughing and yelling to lift the boat with each successive wave higher up the beach till it could be loaded.

It was an amazing sight and Accra could load a ship at a rate of 500 tons of cocoa a day off the beach, while Takoradi, with all its sophisticated lighterage and wharfage could only match the same amount. When bigger pieces of cargo had to be handled, they simply lashed two canoes together, catamaran style, and I have seen them carry ashore reinforcing rods, packing cases, even motor cars.

The other cocoa ports were Winneba, Cape Coast, and Axim though to much lesser degrees. And, until the port of Tema was built near Accra in the late 50's, these ports survived very successfully. Incidentally all of these had been places from which slaves had been shipped in the 18th/19th Centuries. Cape Coast Castle and those of Accra (Danish) Christiansborg and Elmina (Portuguese) had barracoons and deep dungeons to hold the ancestors of the present day West Indian and Afro-American peoples. In addition to these castles there were forts at Axim, Sekondi, Kommenda, Saltpond and at Accra (Fort Orange). All had been built by the various nationalities who had come to explore, plunder and defend for the time they were there, their part of the coast they chose to occupy. This was during the late 17th, 18th and early 19th Centuries – the period of the transatlantic slave trade.

Winneba *approaching the entrance.*

We brought in ships from all over the world, this one was from Amsterdam.

The tug Amrado, twin screw, hard at work.

After three months as a tugmaster in Takoradi, I had become a pilot, docking and undocking 60-70 vessels per month on a rota system to the wharves, buoys, the oil berth and bauxite berth, each of which lay on the weather side of the finger pier and so had to be moored fore and aft by ships' cable to the head buoy and the heavy insurance wire to the after buoy. These in addition to the normal moorings. From September to March was 'Tornado season', when sudden fierce line squalls would come up fast out of the south east and pass over the coast travelling at 35 to 40 knots over the ground.

They were not 'twisters' as experienced in the USA but were line squalls or smallish 'V' depressions full of drenching rain and howling winds, which could tear ships from their moorings and decimate gardens and damage property on shore.

I had only been tugmaster for a week when I found myself towing off the stern of MV *Sekondi* when a line squall struck. All I could see of the ship was my stern tow line disappearing into a drenching mist of rain, while lightning and thunder hissed into the sea around me and boomed overhead. All I could do was hold on and hope that the pilot had let go the anchor. He had. When the

For the auspicious occasion of the opening of the new harbour extension the Amrado, *after a thorough clean-up, took the Governor and his party on their sail-past.*

squall passed, the entire marine staff of pilots, tugmasters and boatmen surveyed the harbour. Seven ships had parted from their stern buoys and lay in a neat echelon to their bow buoys, kept apart from each other only by the log cargos laid between them ready for loading. The wind was still strong south easterly. The Harbour Master asked Robbie, the senior pilot, what we should do. 'I suggest we all go home for breakfast and return when the wind has shifted back to northerly which it'll do in an hour or so.' He was right. By noon all the ships were neatly moored and we were back in business as usual. Every six weeks or so the pilots were in turn to take a tanker from Takoradi ninety miles along the coast to a marine submarine oil terminal some three miles off Accra belonging to Mobil Oil. Mostly the tankers were big (for those days) Scandinavian ships 500 odd feet long, 33 feet draft, 16–18,000, tons. They would call at Takoradi, pick up the pilot about 8 pm and set off for Accra to arrive before daylight. The coastline off Accra had absolutely no distinguishing shore marks, like tall buildings, clumps of trees or even background hills. Completely featureless, it only had the lighthouse of Fort Orange and the Fort, and the low jumble of buildings which comprised the city. The oil berth lay in the sea three miles offshore and a mile and a half to the west of this, marked only by the two

Class II admiralty mooring buoys, painted black, turned to the grey blue of the sea in the dawn by seabird droppings. The radar sets in those days were not as good at picking up small targets like buoys, and add to that a good 6-10 foot swell, and you begin to have some idea of the job.

Once the buoys had been identified it was necessary to approach them from seaward *ie* from the south directly toward the shore, keeping course so as to arrive at the right spot to drop, first the port anchor then the starboard anchor. It is called a running moor, and is normally done in line with a tidal or river current either heading into the stream or running with the stream. But, in order that the ship would lie to the combined effect of tidal current and wind, we had to make the approach at right angles to the tide, spread the anchors, and allow the ship to swing slowly into the tidal current. As she did this four surf canoes had been towed out from Accra beach by a motor launch, each loaded with 1,000, feet of 10 inch nylon rope coiled like a giant snake in the bottom. Each canoe would attach one eye of this rope to the buoy by a giant wooden fid, then, paddling like hell and no notion towards the stern of the ship, would cast out the coils as they came. The crew stood by on the poop with heaving lines and heavier messenger in-lines and it was due mainly to the skill of Norwegian sailors in throwing lines that the ends of these massive ropes were secured so they could be hauled up to the winches. Because all the time the boats paddled, the $2-2^1/_2$ knot current was dragging at the long heavy snake rope in the water. From first dropping anchors at 6 am it took on average $4^1/_2$ hours to secure the stern of the ship by 4 x 10 inch nylon hawsers to these buoys, and adjust her so that the small marker buoy of the underwater flexible was positioned right by the ships' over board discharges. Then the pilot, the agent, and the captain got into one of the canoes and were paddled four miles to the beach, visiting en route any loading ship in Accra anchorage with whom the agent might have business.

Finally came the hair-raising ride to shore through the rolling surf breakers. Each time I did it, I was sure we'd capsize, but always the sure hand of a tall grinning Kroo boy would avert disaster so that we landed in the shallows, to be carried ashore in a surf chair, Canute-like, to land dry shod on the sand. Then it was either a four hour drive back by road or a forty minute flight from Accra to Takoradi.

My seven years in Gold Coast Ghana were spent in the job I have always loved; berthing and un-berthing ships of all sizes and engaging in the administration of a modern port. Mainly humdrum, perhaps, but there were two incidents in which I was instrumental to their success.

Cape St Mary

The first was the rescue of *Cape St Mary*, a Hull trawler of the West African Fisheries Institute (WAFRI), shared by Gambia, Sierra Leone, Ghana and

Nigeria. Manned and mastered by British fishermen, its job was to survey the fisheries of the West African coast.

One day a message came to us from the *St Mary:*

> *50-100 miles south east of Accra. Trawler net foul of propeller.*
> *Please send tug.*

Captain Anderson sent for me and suggested I should take a tug and bring her back. After some discussion we agreed that my friend Nick Trotter, one of our tug masters, should also come. In my mind I knew that Nick's towage experience was greater than mine, as he had come from the Bristol Channel Tug Company, which did both port and sea towage. The tug, *Sir Gordon,* had no lifeboats (taken off to avoid damage when rolling alongside a ship's quarter) and no furnishings in her crew cabins. So Nick and I shared the captain's cabin on the 'hot bunk' system. As he took over from me on the bridge at night, I went below into his nice warm bed. We arranged contact with Takoradi by using radios supplied by our police force to call the various police stations along – Cape Coast Castle, Elmina, Saltpond, Winneba and Accra. We had two steel hawsers of 75 fathoms spliced to be made fast to the tug by a five inch 15 fathom nylon towing spring. Our idea was to connect these hawsers in parallel, shackled into the bow anchor cable of *St Mary.* She would slack her anchor cable down to 1 shackle (fifteen fathoms) ninety feet and so the whole tow line would have plenty of 'spring' for what would likely be a 300 mile tow to safety.

At sunset we left Takoradi for Accra. Nick took first watch with 'Freetown Thomas' as coxwain. We had chosen three of our best steersmen whose knowledge of steering by compass was zero. In port they could always steer by choosing a buoy or cocoa shed to steady on. I went on the bridge and showed Thomas how to steer, not by the lubber line but by the compass card. By midnight we could see the loom of Accra's lights.

We had tried to call each police post on our way, but they did not respond. When we called: 'Accra Police, this is tug boat *Sir Gordon* from Takoradi. Have you any information on *Cape St Mary?*' The only reply we got was from some officer who had obviously not been told about us, talking to another officer, 'Who dis Gordon man? I don know'. So from three miles off Accra lighthouse we set course south east, guessing that *St Mary* would show up in four hours. At midnight I left Nick on watch, asking him to call me after four hours whether he had sighted anything or not. At 4 am he did so, saying 'Wind freshening, nothing to see!' Minutes later we were chatting on the bridge about the weather and how far from *St Mary* could we be, when all at once a brilliant light shone momentarily dead ahead then disappeared. Soon it showed permanently after *St Mary* and ourselves, who had both been plunging up and down in the severe swell, were happy to see each other plainly.

As dawn broke I cruised round the trawler to see that her trawl net was well wound up in her propeller and rudder. The ship had broken the anchor cable at the first shackle and was ready to accept our 'twin' wire hawsers shackled securely to her anchor cable. By her design as a trawler, she was lying abeam to the heavy swell, so we decided to approach her from upwind, and I would cross her bows at right angles very close to, so that her anchor cable could be caught by our crewmen and shackled swiftly to our hawsers.

I approached the trawler with the wind dead astern. Nick stood on the fantail of the tug, the crew ready to throw or catch heaving lines. As I passed the bow of the trawler I could almost have reached out and touched her plunging stem. But in moments we were passing and the anchor cable was almost in the hands of Nick, who used his skill and courage to secure our tow lines and throw the rest into the sea.

I allowed *Sir Gordon* to drift under the wind for the full length of the tow rope lines, and just as the tow stretched out we heard the screaming wind of the line squall. Drenching rain lost our sight of the trawler, but stretching into the wild gloom we could see and 'feel' the tow line holding on. Two and a half days later, after having to use the 'big tank' of the sea to top up the boilers, we got back safely, but drenched and cold to Takoradi.

The British Commander

The second incident occurred one Saturday afternoon when I was scheduled to take a tanker off the oil berth and replace her with another, the *British Commander*, a 12,000 ton BP vessel, due to arrive at 1500 hrs. Just as we were casting off the last lines Bill Todman, our Harbour Master shouted from the jetty: 'David, your arrival tanker has run ashore at the back of the breakwater. I'll join you on the pilot launch'.

I was astonished to see the *British Commander* well up almost alongside an old wreck who, many years ago, had dropped her pilot at the entrance and instead of steering three miles to the fairway buoy had turned hard round the end of the breakwater and right up on to the reef.

Captain Todman and I went round in the pilot boat to where the stranded vessel lay. We read the draft both fore and aft. She should have been 28'6", what we read was thirty feet aft and twenty-six feet forward. We boarded the ship and spoke to the Captain, somewhat embarrassed in that he had been having the usual Sunday custom on these ships, namely, inviting all non-duty officers to his cabin, leaving the third officer on watch as they approached Takoradi.

We got the mate and carpenter to take soundings right round the vessel, while we discussed the possibility of the heavy swell pounding the ship on the hard coral reef. I felt the ship lift and fall on the swell as if she were pinioned by a lump of coral under her foremast. Her cargo was kerosene in the forward

The Clyde Pioneer *taking off the* British Commander's *cargo, enabling her to be re-floated at high tide.*

tanks and petrol in her after tanks. The Captain and I argued, for I wanted to lighten the ship by discharging some of her no. 7 tanks from under the foremast, eventually he agreed, reluctantly, to do so.

While this was being arranged, we got the tug *Takoradi* bollard pull of 15 tons to connect up with the insurance wire of *Commander* – seventy-five fathoms of it – and pulling off on the starboard quarter, to hope that the ship's head would slowly swing back to 350°, which was the head when she ran aground at 1500 hr. Captain Todman and I went on to the poop and anxiously watched her lift and pound as the swell increased after sunset at 1800 hr. From the way she was working and creaking, we felt she could split in two and that would mean a 12,999 ton pollution of the Gold Coast and probably a huge fire. As high water approached, the pull of *Takoradi* was having the effect of the compass head moving slowly back through north and to her original grounding course. The range of tide on the coast was only 6·5 feet. We had the main engines working at 'full astern' for the last two hours towards High Water. We kept a good eye on the compass head. Suddenly she swung to 350° and the engine room signalled by a 'double ring astern'. At the same moment *Takoradi* gave three blasts of her siren and our shore bearings began to change. We were afloat, and anchored three miles off shore.

The next day we berthed *British Commander* at the oil berth and she was tested for underwater damage, finding fourteen leaks in her cargo tanks. Five days later a sister vessel, *Clyde Pioneer*, recently discharged from Lagos came in and berthed alongside *Commander* on running moor and stern-on to the oil berth, separated by fenders of five mahogany logs, holding them apart, but workable. Both ships sailed in another five days and that was the end of what could have been a disastrous episode.

Collision

When we were leaving Takoradi in August 1957, I had to report to the main headquarter of Ghana Railways and take my inventory of all my furniture and Railway goods in our bungalow. As I said my farewells to my Ghana Railway friends I was greeted by one of the Old Africans. 'We are sorry to see you go', he said, 'Africans taking over the railways are not good compared with you white men'. And as I shook his hand, there were tears in his eyes.

In my latter years I had become a member of the enquiry committee which investigated any railway incidents. The entire railway ran on 36" gauge rails together with speed limits of 40 mph on the numerous bends. When a 120 ton double ended loco pulling a thousand tons of manganese came round a bend at 60 mph, it struggled against centrifugal force and hurtled into the bush. Each time we set up an enquiry the engine crews swore blind that they were travelling inside the limit, and we had to prove, through the damaged tracks and overturned wagons that they had been untruthful.

One time the loco had collided with a juju cottonwood tree of an eight foot diameter and standing eighty feet tall. The local villagers gathered round to say to Ghana Railways management that the juju spirit that lived in the tree wanted thanks for no one being killed. I had to go as the railway representative and talk to the head man of the village. I got some good advice from the African General Manager. 'Take two bottles of gin and a large basket of fruits, and hold a special meeting on a full moon evening'. From various advice from friends, what I did gave satisfaction. With the head man and myself holding each a gin bottle and a village crowd around us, we stood together before the damaged tree trunk and making appropriate gestures, we poured a good slug of gin on the wood. Then we each had a tipple and passed the bottles round the folk. It was a success.

CHAPTER 5
LOOKING BACK AT GOLD COAST ORIGINS

By 1471 the Portuguese were at the Gold Coast. Their mariners, who had learned to master the ocean in the hard school of the Atlantic fisheries made that first contact with Black Africa in 1444 when they reached Cape Verde and the mouth of the Senegal and began to colonise the Cape Verde Islands.

At the Gold Coast, they found so much gold that in 1482 at Elmina, some forty miles east from Takoradi/Sekondi, they began the first series of coastal ports, designed to include other European seafarers now following in their wake, in its profitable trade.

Slavery in Africa had existed since the 9th Century onwards. It is not my intention nor do I have the time to go into such a massive subject here and now. The Portuguese developing their new colony of Brazil desperately needed labour. What better to do than join in the flourishing trade and develop the Atlantic slave trade which was to spread from Angola north through Nigeria, Dahomey, Gold and Ivory Coasts up to Senegal, overseas to West Indies and the new American colonies.

During the 17th/18th Centuries competition for this trade was fierce as it affected Gold Coast, between Portugal, the Dutch, the Danes and British. The British won eventually and ended up with Gold Coast and Trans Volta Togoland.

Then of course the trade in slaves was a great incentive. Many of the great families of England, their houses and their wealth depended on this dreadful traffic in human misery. But by 1865 England had decided to abolish this trade and pursued slavers using special naval frigates for the purpose, and by the end of the 19th Century the Gold Coast had come under the administration of the Colonial Office, based on the style of India, with a Governor, Civil Service, District Officers and efficient Public Works Department. District Officers were extremely wise, experienced men who gained the confidence of local chiefs and village headmen. Under this fairly enlightened system of British Rule, the country was run through the tribal system which was overseen by the District Officers who in turn answered the Governor in Accra.

Most of these Governors were very good administrators, who reigned – that is the word – as Sovereign's Representative in truly regal splendour. Some of their names spring to mind, brought to life in the naming of marine craft of the Harbour Board. *Sir Ransford Slater* (a tug), *Lady Slater* (a pilot boat), *Sir Gordon Guggisberg* (a bigger tug), and so on.

During our time the Governor was Sir Charles Arden-Clarke, and a most imposing figure he made on the podium in his uniform decorations and plumed helmet, as he stood to take the homage of the paramount chiefs and lesser chiefs and headmen at the local Durbar of Eastern province, held on Takoradi Airfield every five years.

The Atlantic Charter made between President Roosevelt and Churchill on board a warship in August 1941 undertook that, when the war was won they would:

> *Respect the right of all peoples to choose the form of government*
> *under which they will live.*

Thousands of African volunteers, – with far more conscripts, joined in a war which they understood as in their Swahili propaganda message Vita via uhure 'a war for freedom'.

Nine brigades were raised in West Africa alone. And there is no doubt that when they came home having seen a lot of the outside world that they wanted nothing but freedom.

The Rise Of Nationalism

At the end of World War II all of the allied colonial powers seemed capable of holding on to their possessions. This was to be revealed as an illusion. As the battles ended and the soldiers returned home, great changes of opinion and interest were at work. The first clear sign of this was small in size but large in influence. The event occurred in 1948 at a sleepy crossroads in Accra, capital of Britain's 'model colony' of West Africa, the Gold Coast, where indeed any overt sign of change was least expected. The symbol of the crossroads was to acquire a continental meaning.

From the walls of the great white castle of Christiansborg where the Governor lived, a little road, Castle Drive, led to the intersection for Accra. Today it was peaceful and empty as usual. It was about 3 pm on a hot clammy afternoon. But, down at the crossroads, quite unusually, stood a posse of armed African police under command of a British Inspector. They were waiting for trouble though still hoping to avoid it. Then there appeared the head of a column of some 2,000 marchers from the town, walking on a route which had been forbidden by the police. All were unarmed but were marching well, for they were veteran ex-servicemen of the Gold Coast Brigade that had fought so well against Italian Fascist armies in East Africa and later against the Japanese in Burma. Led by former sergeants and wearing their campaign medals they were carrying a petition concerned with grievances over jobs and war pensions which they hoped to present to the Governor. They were resolute and pushed against the handful of police. The British Inspector rather lost his head and ordered tear gas, but the wind was wrong and the crowd responded with a hail of stones. The inspector snatched a rifle from one of his men, killing a former sergeant and a youth and wounding several others. The marchers who had no intentions of such violence turned back.

The reaction throughout the Gold Coast was immediate. Riots in Kumasi, Cape Coast, Takoradi and other smaller towns over three days. Eventually things settled down, but the 'massacre at the crossroads' remained in African memories. Later when Kwame Nkrumah had won independence the first memorial to be constructed was at the crossroads and stands today a magnificent Portland Stone arch over Independence Avenue inscribed with the words 'Freedom and Justice'.

The Governor's reaction to the riots was of course predictable. Although Nkrumah, lately arrived from the USA after eight years at various universities, had no part in the affair he along with six other prominent leaders of the United Gold Coast Convention (UGCC), as it was known, were arrested on the grounds that they were promoting a Communist plot. This charge of course could not stick, and a court of inquiry had them all released.

Nkrumah quickly broke from UGCC and formed his own Convention People's Party (CPP) a much more dynamic political movement, with many local branches, lists of members, designs for demonstrations, strikes or anything else that could be useful short of violence.

In 1951 a general election was held and CPP had an overwhelming victory, soon becoming the party of government, still under a British Governor Sir James Arden-Clarke until 1957 when on 7th March the Duke of Edinburgh attended the Independence Ceremonies in Christiansborg Castle and the Union Flag of Britain was lowered for the last time and the red, gold and green flag of the new Ghana hoisted in its place. The five-pointed black star symbolises the United Government of the Gold Coast, the five territories of Ghana – the Western Province, Eastern Province, Northern Territories, VOLTA and Trans Volta Togoland. The colours stand for the blood of Africans shed in the past, the golden sands of the desert (Northern Territories) and the green of the forests.

Ghana was the first country of black Africa to achieve independence after World War II. Red, yellow and green stripes appeared on the flag, these being the original colours of Ethiopia, the oldest independent African state. These colours have become the so called Pan-African colours which vary slightly in symbolism from country to country.

On the Ghanian flag:

RED stands for the blood of the heroes who fell during the struggle for freedom.

The new flag of Ghana.

YELLOW represents the mineral wealth, particularly gold, which gave its name to the Gold Coast.

GREEN is for the country's forests and fertile fields. The BLACK five-pointed star represents:

NT   Northern Territories Ashanti
EP   East Province
WP   West Province
TVT   Trans Volta Togoland

On 7th March 1957 Kwame Nkrumah was installed as President of Ghana at a wonderful, joyous celebration in Accra, our capital.

Almost at once a process called 'Africanisation' was begun. If an African could possibly replace a British Colonial Officer in any part of the Administration, be it administrative, clerical, financial or technical, out went the European. So far as the Marine Department was concerned we could not yet be replaced as qualified expert pilots and tugmasters, but the writing was on the wall.

We left in late 1957 on board *Aureol* after seven and a half years of one of the most interesting and happy periods of our lives. The Ghana people we found to be a cheerful friendly polite people, with very close tribal and family ties. Even today, sometimes when I see a coloured smiling face, I expect to hear the jovial greeting 'Ha – I see you my friend'.

CHAPTER SIX

THE WATERS OF TYNE

When we came home to England after seven years in Ghana I went back to British Rail at Heysham for just over a year. I kept my eye on Lloyds List, that wonderful newsy newspaper. Apart from news of ships all over the world, it carried many advertisements for marine jobs.

In 1960 I was appointed Ferries Superintendent to the Tyne Improvement Commission, managing the three famous ferries which ran from North Shields to South Shields at fifteen minute intervals, the *Tynemouth, Northumbria* and the *South Shields*.

There were three masters, three relief masters and three foremen. The whole system worked on three eight-hour shifts, the night shift from 11pm till 7am looked after the ferries moored at North and South landings with the 'spare' boat also at South landing.

Since they were coal burners, they were coaled every morning alternately. The service was started from 7am till 7pm. Each ferry carried a good number of vehicles, and when the shipyards changed shifts, morning and evening, they carried five hundred people at a time.

The only time we reduced service was in the dense fog which frequently occurred and often the dry docks on both sides of the Tyne could have the river full of large tankers, each with four tugs manoeuvring her. Fortunately each ferry was fitted with a Decca Radar of intense clarity.

One severe winter, the Tyne was frozen for many miles upstream. When the thaw came in March, Shields harbour was filled with blocks of ice over which scampered the odd rabbit or hare. The running ferries had all their paint 'between wind and water' scrubbed off to 'bright steel'. In the basin of South Shields fishmarket the ice heaved up and down and my young daughter remarked: 'Dad, the ice is breathing,' and indeed that was how it looked.

Every week I went from North Shields to the Tyne Improvement Commission in Newcastle to collect the wages for the ferries staff. My office was on the first floor of a narrow, three storey building from where I had the most magnificent outlook both up and down the Tyne. From my windows I could keep an eye on both landings and all that went on, ferry-wise; also the wonderful panorama of the Tyne entrance with its famous piers stretching out into the North Sea.

The well remembered Tyne ferry.

One summer morning an eighty-thousand ton tanker who had been out on her trials was coming in on a flood tide. All of a sudden I heard a lot of launch and small ship whistles blowing and I went to the window. Our ferry on North Landing had just let go early and moved off into the river. The vast bow and bulk of the tanker was heading straight for the landing stage, despite the efforts of the tugs.

Miraculously the stern tug had pulled the stern so much that the bow just cleared the landing, but as the ship slipped past, the water ballast which she was discharging poured out like a tremendous waterfall over the landing; one of the securing anchor cables gave a great crack and was totally broken. It could so easily have been a terrible disaster.

The top storey of the long narrow building was the Harbour Master's office. There were two deputy Harbour Masters, one of whom took a harbour patrol launch and cruised up river to Newcastle every day. There he would go to the office in Gateshead and write up what he had seen in the way of shipping, shipyards and any marine problems in the river.

Each ferry was manned – on deck – by the captain, who handled the ship across Shields harbour, with two deck hands and – in the engine room – a 'chief' who drove and lubricated the engines while two firemen kept the furnaces going, using their years of firing skill to keep the smoke from the funnel at a minimum, particularly at the South Landing, where at low tide, the funnel height was that of South Shields main street.

The Clean Air Act had recently come in and the busy housewives in South Shields were not slow to complain about the ferry smoke, so we had to extend the funnels of all the ferries by about six feet in order to raise the height of the offending smoke.

The natural consequence of coal firing.

Once or twice the senior foreman would bring to my office a fireman for a 'carpeting' due to carelessness in firing at South Landing. I might threaten to dismiss him, but not often, because it was difficult to get 'coal burning men' as they were becoming increasingly scarce.

Each landing had a man to help tie up the boats and assist any passengers who might need help. At the top of each bridge to the landing stood the ticket office where the fares were collected from small cars to eight ton lorries which would be held to one side until all twenty-six cars were on board; then the lorry would be guided carefully on to the cross deck and the foreman would make sure the brakes were secure.

The High Lights and the Low Lights at the mouth of the Tyne. An original watercolour of 1920.

Passengers had to pay the collector, whose little office controlled the turn-stile, which sometimes a rush of five hundred shipyard men would try to force. The fare was 'three ha'pence' and the smartie-pants man who would present a ten-shilling note through the pigeon hole was given his change in a tightly rolled coil of coppers. With hundreds of his fellow workers pressing behind him, our collectors had a good reputation. All their money was brought upstairs into my general office, checked and banked the following day.

On our evening ferry boat, the 7pm from North to South carried the 'ladies' of the town, whose base was a large imposing house on the river front a hundred yards from the ferry station, known as 'The Jungle'. The 7.15pm boat, on return to North Shields would carry the Southern Belles to parade their wares there. The last trip of the ferry would exchange the 'ladies' back to their own parts.

When the Powers that Be decided to build a tunnel under the Tyne it meant that there would be no more vehicle ferries and I was advised to look for another appointment.

Thus it was that I came to Whitby.

CHAPTER SEVEN

WHITBY (i)

Whitby town is an ancient town
Near a wide and sandy shore,
And ships have sailed from the little port
A thousand years or more . . .

On a June evening in 1964 nine seafarers met together in the offices of Whitby Urban District Council in their handsome surroundings in St Hilda's Terrace, looking out over the town.

As we waited, we all chatted and exchanged experiences as to what we had done and where we had been. As has always been in my life we were chosen in alphabetical order, so I was almost last. I recalled, as I waited, the last time I had appeared before a corporation, some thirty councillors sitting in a hollow square with my seat at the centre of a U shaped group which made me feel like a prisoner at the bar.

Whitby was different. A handsome semi-circle of desks and chairs with the chairman and town clerk facing them and I was invited to sit beside them on the empty chair. For about three quarters of an hour I was quizzed about my career and how I would run a harbour. A short list of three of us went back to the waiting room for some ten minutes. Since one of them was the Deputy Harbour Master, we both thought he would be selected, but he said, 'Oh it's not like that here, some of these councillors have their own ideas.'

When I was called back into the council chamber the Chairman welcomed me as the new Harbour Master of Whitby. I stood with him at the door as all eighteen councillors filed past and either shook my hand and gave their congratulations or simply walked past with a grunt and 'Good night.'

I did wonder what I had let myself in for, but the clerk of the council told me that all would be well. I rejoined my wife in the car park and went home happy.

We had to live on a temporary basis in a council house, kindly given by the council, whilst we got settled in our own house, 'Cliffhaven' on the West Cliff where we have lived for some thirty years.

I began my new occupation on 12th August 1964, exactly twenty-four years from my first day at sea. The Deputy Harbour Master had to go into hospital

Whitby Harbour.

within a week, so I was left in a brand new job to take up the reins of operating a small but busy port in north east Yorkshire, famous for its association with Captain Cook, whose bronze statue stands on the West Cliff overlooking the harbour and gazing out to sea.

Part of the Harbour Master's appointment included being Pilot Master, under Trinity House in Newcastle upon Tyne. I had been told by the Deputy Harbour Master that apart from High Tide, the tidal stream ran across the harbour bar, so that any vessel entering the harbour between the piers would find her bow out of the tidal current and her stern being swung strongly towards the East Pier and at the same time to push the bow away from the West Pier extension end. So as a vessel had pointed directly towards the West Pier extension, the helm had to be ordered hard to port. This had the effect of turning the bow of the ship away from the West Bullnose Pier and at the same time to push the stern away from the East Pier. Thus a ship would enter the two piers safely; a tricky and difficult manoeuvre, but part of the skill of the ship's pilot.

My first ship was a small 150 foot long vessel come to load limestone cargo at the north end of the fish quay. Called *Reedwarbler*, I was to bring her into Jeddah, Saudi Arabia, many years later under an Arabic name, *Arafat*.

ii WHITBY REGATTA

Less than a fortnight after taking up my appointment as Harbour Master I gathered from my staff that it was to be Regatta weekend and I was to be in charge of all the stalls which would be erected along Pier Road right to the end of the pier. Fortunately for me, the Whitby Urban District employed a 'Council Constable' whose duties included guarding the person of the Mayor of Whitby, generally keeping an eye on the streets and properties of the town. This was Les Stainthorpe and I had a talk with him about the Regatta.

'A lot of these fairground folk will call on you and ask for a place,' he told me, 'When they come, I'll be around if you don't mind, Sir.' I did not mind. On my first Regatta Saturday the lobby of Pier House had a dozen or so such people.

Just as I wondered what to do, Les appeared in his smart uniform. He quietened down the hubbub and said, 'Now you lot. Just listen to me. Here is the new Harbour Master. What he says, goes. If any one of you gets out of line he'll call me and I'll tell you wherever you are on the pier – you can just fold your tent and steal away!'

On Regatta Sunday many rowing races were held between the two rival clubs, the Fisherman's Rowing Club and the Whitby Amateur Rowing Club. They had both practised for weeks before and the stentorian tones of the coxes urging the crews on could be heard from the vantage points on the West Cliff on many an evening. The races were held from outside the harbour and into Whitby Bridge. I think the longest race was from Newholm Beck, then from a point opposite Black Steps near Upgang Ravine. But I could never watch the finals because of fair stalls.

On the Sunday evening scores of stall vehicles collected outside the Royal Hotel under the watchful eye of the police. At 6 pm all traffic along Pier Road was stopped and barricades erected by the police. At 9 pm myself, my Deputy Harbour Master and my Harbour Foreman waited outside the Yacht Club whilst our police officer radioed to the top of the Pass and the wagons were allowed down slowly in groups of eight at a time. Those who had a place far out along the West Pier came in the first convoy as well as some who stood on Battery Parade. The King family, a group of fortune telling caravans, took up part of Scotch Head and so on and so on. They came down until around midnight and were checked off on our lists until 100-120 stalls were ready for the morning. Many disturbances were created between stallholders. For example, each stall was paid for at a rate of so much per ten foot space. Two such adjoining spaces would be allocated, but one would have 'wings' which would encroach on the other.

On Pier Road I had to set them up behind a chalk line to keep the road and pavement clear for the hundreds of people who would frequent the various stalls, from 'Roll a Penny' to 'Bows and Arrows' and cowboy hats, and from large china ware and blanket stalls, usually under the roof of the Fishmarket.

Battery Parade was usually taken up by the Mason family. One year in the first eight down Mr Mason cleared himself and his truck for Battery; but in the second eight was Mrs Mason. 'All right,' I said, 'Your husband has already gone down.' Her language was a blast of rude words from which I gathered that she was no longer married to Mr Mason. They had divorced in the last year. 'Go round and tell him that I say he should share the thirty foot space.' She went off, still fuming.

I always carried a tape measure and chalk and I went to the Battery Parade about an hour later. The noise was awful. Mr Mason was shouting at his wife whilst Mrs Mason's fourteen-year old boy was fiercely attacking his Dad, fists and

Whitby Regatta, the Commodore's sail past.

feet going hammer and tongs into Mason's stout belly. When they saw my uniform, things eased off. In silence I measured off two fifteen foot lengths, marked the border heavily in chalk and turned to Mrs Mason. 'You shall choose the one you want and you, Mr Mason will have the other. If you don't agree and I hear any more, you will both close!' How I could have done that I don't know.

Every year the stall management was full of incidents. Once a round stall was set up half way along the West Pier selling nylon stockings which were picked up by the westerly breeze parachute fashion and deposited over the railings, into the mud of the harbour. Another time a veritable pantechnicon came in the first eight. One side of it was painted in ghouls and ghosts and on the same side was a cake walk. Mr Gooch, a little man, explained to me how he hid in the various corridors and blew whistles and touched two electric wires to illuminate grinning ghostly faces. About an hour later two Regatta Committee men came to me and said that one or two ladies who had gone into the ghost bus had complained that someone inside the labyrinth was rudely touching them. I had to walk the length of the pier through dense crowds to where Gooch was standing outside his cake walk.

'Mr Gooch,' I said, 'you can close up all this. – You'll know why.'

'Oh! All right,' he said, 'but can I open my 'Slave Girl'?'

His slave girl was his sixteen year old blondie daughter in a ten-foot square tent. 'OK' I said 'but I'll be along to see her.' When I called back there was a small crowd who were complaining about the charge of sixpence. Inside the tent was a roped off square in which lay a young girl in a black bikini on a pile of straw. Over her ankles and wrists were some bits of rusty chain. She was reading a comic. Her comments about her father were not very polite.

At ten o'clock on the Monday morning the Regatta Treasurer and I started from the Marine Hotel and worked our way very slowly to the end of the West Pier, collecting with some difficulty but determination the rents for each stall, making around twelve hundred pounds which, at that time, paid for the fireworks display that evening. A splendid show to end the Regatta.

iii   THE PILOTAGE OF WHITBY

The pilotage of Whitby under Newcastle-upon-Tyne Trinity House required knowledge a bit more than pointing the ship between the piers. A ship would be boarded off the Buoy which was 0·8 miles from the Pier Extension Ends. It marked the edge of Whitby Rock and all ships in the North Sea kept to seaward side of it. Then if approaching the entrance, always kept well to the westward of the Rock. Three cables inshore of the buoy the Rock protruded in a small Diamond Head over which the sea would break with a treacherous sea particularly for smaller boats.

The final thing to watch was the tidal stream which on flood tide was always strong from west to east across the harbour mouth, tending to sweep the vessel on to the East Extension End.

During my fourteen years in Whitby some three thousand cargo ships were piloted in and out of the port and of them only two nudged the East Extension Pier and one could not respond to her rudder and ended up fifteen feet from the Burgess Pier and fast aground, requiring tugs from the Tees to refloat her.

Pilotage could be done in northerly winds up to Force 5 to 6 Beaufort Scale which could create quite heavy breakers entering the harbour.

One winter night a Norwegian ship called *Reitan* anchored in Sandsend Bay on her first visit to Whitby. High water was 2 am and even as I went out for the ship a blizzard came down and it was only through our radar and the ship's deck lights that we were able to find her. It was difficult to move the ship on an Easterly course and try to find the lights of the town, apart from the red and green Pier lights. One of the red lights which led right through the entrance was mounted in the street lamp standard half way up the 199 steps which led from Church Street to St Mary's Church. One red light which was not a recognised navigation light was a lamp which a fisherman's wife put in the front window of her house whose position looked right down the fairway of the harbour mouth.

With the aid of the pilot cutter who kept herself just far enough ahead of the ship so that the bridge of the ship (*ie* the pilot) could see the light of the Aldis lamp of the cutter. And with good luck and God's help and our own skill 'Reitan' was brought safely into her haven.

Whitby Pilots.

Watching the safe unloading of cargo.

iv THE LIFE BOAT

During the last four years of being Harbour Master I became Honorary Secretary and Launching Authority to Whitby's long lived lifeboat, the *Mary Ann Hepworth*, which today is still run by one of her ex-crew taking tourist trips into the bay from Scotch Head steps.

The RNLI were offered the cost of a new, self righting lifeboat by a lady called Gwyneth Milburn. The Waveney boat was christened at a wonderful ceremony on Scotch Head by the Duchess of Kent and named appropriately *The White Rose of Yorkshire* to serve Whitby for ten years.

Whilst the *Mary Ann Hepworth* had been manned by eight, older traditional fishermen of Whitby, *White Rose* gradually changed her crew to five younger, more technical young men with an experienced fisherman as their coxwain. Any time she went to sea the general public watched her till she disappeared into the bad weather.

We also had an inshore lifeboat, manned by the members of the lifeboat crew of some twelve young men and they did some wonderful, dangerous inshore rescues under the East Cliff. Once, when the weather was North West Force 7, with seas breaking into Saltwick Bay, the Coastguard called me to say a man was trapped by the tide below the Coastguard Station. I ordered the inshore lifeboat to go out and try to reach the man. They got inside the big rocks just offshore, dropped their anchor and veered down on to the beach. Two crew men stayed in the boat while one went through the water and persuaded the sixteen-stone man to come into the cold water and be helped into the rubber dinghy. The seas were very rough and as they pulled away from the beach into deeper water, the anchor rope snapped and the boat up-ended and all of them were thrown back on the beach. The dinghy hull was punctured and thrown ashore beside them.

I launched No.1 boat with the knowledge that her twin screw hull could not get close in, but she could fire her rocket line to shore, but alas, the wind just blew it adrift.

Facing page: The White Rose of Yorkshire *crossing the bar and proving her sea-worthiness.*

By this time I had been invited to go to the Coastguard Station at the top of the cliff. The Coastguard officer and I decided to send a Coastguard to be abseiled down the cliff, carrying over his shoulders a portable rocket apparatus. Once again the fickle wind would not allow the rocket line near enough for the *White Rose* men to grasp it.

Had this been done, the broken inshore lifeboat and crew could have been pulled to safety by the big lifeboat – herself in among dangerous rocks. High water was approaching and the men on the beach could be drowned. We decided to ask for the RAF rescue helicopter from Leeming. It would take twenty minutes. Just before High Water the chopper arrived and picked up the five men one at a time and landed them beside us on top of the cliff. With the very strong north wind blowing the helicopter against the 200 feet cliff, we could see that at times the whirling blades could be as close as fifty feet to inevitable disaster.

Next day the sixteen stone man called at the Coastguard Station to ask why no one had gone back for his anorak.

Facing page top: *After the loss of the inshore lifeboat Miss Milner presented a new one to the RNLI. This was named after its donor who is shown here at its launch with Lord and Lady Normanby, Whitby's RNLI chairman Alan Marshall and the Honorary RNLI secretary David Stevenson. The* White Rose of Yorkshire *is in the background.*
Facing page bottom: *Crews from both vessels attended the launch.* **L to R back:** *Richard Robinson, Tony Easton, Barry Mason, Neil Williamson, Brian Hodgson, Dave Wharton, Dave Chubb.* **Front:** *Pete Turner, Miss Milburn, Mike Coates.*

v WHITBY BRIDGE

Whitby Bridge was built in 1910 by Messers Heenan & Froude of Manchester. The engineer was Mitchell Moncrieffe. By now it must be one of the last double leaf swing bridges in everyday use for both vehicle and pedestrian traffic. It is operated both electrically and hydraulically. First, locking bolts are taken out, then the two halves slowly swing open. Meanwhile all cross town traffic has stopped, save for that crossing the new bridge farther upstream.

The bridge has had many moods and 'swings' of fortune. A particular occasion comes to mind. From Archangel a Polish vessel took a sheer towards the Marine Hotel area of the Fish Quay and had to let go her anchor to check and pull up. She then hove up. The pilot got the 'all clear' from the bow, proceeded through the bridge. The anchor, not clear, caught the power cables on the bottom. There was a flash and a bang in the Bridge House and the whole thing caught fire. When all had cleared the cable was found on the anchor flukes. The bridge had to be operated in hand gear for a week till a new cable was supplied and relaid.

Whitby Bridge, one of the last double-leaf swing bridges in daily use.

The biggest failure occurred sometime in the winter of the late 1960's. On attempting to close the East Leaf a horrid grinding noise was heard from underneath, and the locking bolts just would not come anywhere near to closing. The main casting which held the spur drive axle in place had a great diagonal crack in it. The Borough Engineer and his team together with the Harbour Master and his team cogitated, and found that by the use of six Acrow building jacks and wooden wedges the bracket could be held in place and the bridge closed in safety.

We had a pow-wow in the Bridge House and phoned various Engineering Companies, ACD Bridge Company, Cleveland Bridge & Engineering Company, Dorman Long. Not one was interested. Then Captain Cook had an idea. 'Remember first principles' he said. 'The bridge is steel – the ships are steel, let's try our shipyard'. Our shipyard at the time was Kindbergs of West Hartlepool a tiny outfit in Hartlepool Dock on the very berth where the 'Warrior' was fitted out and where the 'Trincomalee' was refitted. They came to Whitby, surveyed the job, we gave them our parameters. They said 'OK we can do it, give us three weeks'. And by golly they were as good as their word. Within the time limit a new casting was fabricated and fitted. No traffic or shipping disruption was caused. Total cost £3,000.

I reported the facts to the Council. One councillor said 'I move that congratulations are in order to———'. He was interrupted brusquely by the Harbour Committee Chairman who said 'Out of order – I move next business!' I could not contain my feelings. I knew I would be 'Out of order' but I had to say: 'Thank you Mr Chairman. I shall pass your comments on to those concerned. I'm sure they will be impressed!'

vi   DREDGER ESK

In 1936 Whitby Urban District Council bought the dredger *Esk* at a cost of £8,000. Thirty years later the loan was paid off. In earlier years the Esk had been laid up on the Bell Shoal for part of the year and dredged the harbour only so long as the money she had earned on hire lasted. (In those three decades almost every part of her steel structure had been replaced or renewed).

By 1964 *Esk* was on a regular three months hire to Bridlington Harbour Commissioners and had other short hirings to Hartlepool, Seaham Harbour and Smiths Dock on the Tees to clear their dock entrances. In response to requests from the Fishermens' & Boatmens' Society and the Sea Fisheries Committee we instituted a regular programme of monthly harbour channel and bar soundings while the *Esk* carried out a regular dredging programme of the harbour. The sounding printouts were made available at every Harbour Committee, to be perused by the fishing representative and any councillors. The *Esk* was removing some 93,000 tons of spoil annually from the harbour as well as drawing old piles out of the bed of the harbour, and many other varied marine tasks. Once while dredging Hartlepool Coal Staithes she recovered enough good clean coal to keep her cook stove going for an indefinite period, saving ratepayers money – though we couldn't tell anyone about it!

In the years 1967-77 Whitby seemed to flourish as a port. Fish landings kept increasing, as new boats kept appearing. From 62 vessels in 1962 cargo trade had increased to around 250 vessels per year. Yachts and pleasure craft increased in numbers from 120 in 1964 to around 400. Whitehall Shipyard under Mr Keith Schellenberg had exciting and innovative plans for improvement and attracting yachts and people to the area.

Sadly these somehow failed in the actuality of their fruition. For a time the Shipyard Club, with its Whaler Bar, Boutique and Restaurant, Fashion Shows on the Fish Quay, and power boat racing roused extreme interest but they faded away. Schellenberg left, and the Whitehall Yard passed into the scene it is today of complete desolation.

Perhaps the meeting of minds between Scarborough Borough Council and Yorkshire Water Authority will prove beneficial, though time keeps passing with little visible result.

Here perhaps is the place to describe my vision of Full Council Meetings as they were, and I have little reason to suppose they have altered much.

Whitby Urban District Council meetings were held once a month at 6.45 pm on Thursdays. All council officers had to attend and to sit at a table to one side of the chamber, next to the reporters from the *Whitby Gazette*. We were allowed no comment, unless we had been given notice of a particular question, but we could be criticised most severely by councillors and defended or not as our particular chairman thought fit. Many a stormy evening went on in that chamber. The man who took it all most phlegmatically was Public Health Officer Harry Eatough, who always brought along a magazine and calmly read it throughout the proceedings.

Tactics which most of the officers employed in order to influence any discussion taking place were either to nod steadily in agreement if a councillor on his feet was talking sense or shake his head slowly, and definitely with the appropriate expression of outrage, horror or dismay. Sometimes it worked. We liked to think so, and in any case, it helped to pass the time.

In 1974 Local Government Reorganisation came into being, with its promise of leaner, less expensive, more efficient services to everyone.

Where do we hear these words today?

The experience did not bear out the promise and Whitby Urban District Council found itself, along with Whitby Rural District Council, Filey, Scalby and other smaller districts gobbled up into greater Scarborough Borough Council. Slowly and inevitably the power and authority which had been vested in Whitby people, was whittled away – sometimes drastically – sometimes in more subtle ways, but always taking away from Whitby until today when almost total control is vested in Scarborough.

Today the picture in Whitby Harbour is not bright. Partly due to the recession partly to other factors, shipping traffic is sporadic and sparse. The fishing industry has tremendous problems, due to over fishing and due to Government Policy – or lack of one! Whitehall Shipyard is a wilderness of dereliction and a disgrace to a proud tradition. Its only hope lies in becoming a housing development. But! 'Fiumus and Sumus' is Whitby's motto. I would like to add a last word 'Erimus.'

We were, we are, (and we will be).

CHAPTER EIGHT

THE PORT OF JEDDAH IN SAUDI ARABIA

After my fourteen years as Harbour Master, originally under Whitby Urban District Council, I had a good reputation as one who could manage the wonderfully famous port of Whitby, the local government became re-organised. In our area the three towns of Whitby, Scarborough and Filey were merged into one joint authority and called Scarborough Borough Council. Taken over by Scarborough, the number of councillors from each town was restricted to six members from Filey and six from Whitby. Today it is in the proportion of three from Filey, eight from Whitby and Scarborough bringing the total up to forty-nine members. Personnel like myself were classed as 'middle management' and when I asked the Chief Executive Officer what that meant he said: 'So far as you are concerned, David, just do as you have always done, so long as you report when asked by administration all will go well.'

In the first few months of 'Scarborough', the Chief Executive and the 'big four' visited Whitby and Filey to inspect and adjust things that they felt could be improved.

My visit was by the Chief Executive on his own. I met him on Scotch Head, by the bandstand and we crossed the road to the Harbour Office. As we entered the vestibule his eye was caught by the Whitby Coat of Arms in a nice varnished glass case. I had obtained this from the ship brokers offices which had been the public library at Dock End, and they had no use for the plaque. I thought it was a good idea to have the lovely Coat of Arms in the Harbour Office.

'What are these things doing in Scarborough's Office?' the Chief Executive barked out. 'They can't stay there any more!' My reply was brief and to the point. 'If you read the Latin inscription it says 'Fiumus et Sumus', which means 'We were and We are,' I said. 'We should have added Et Erimus – And we shall be.'

'What is more,' I said stiffly, 'I have to tell you that that Coat of Arms will remain in this office as long as I remain Harbour Master.'

'Hrrmph' he grunted, and left soon after to return to Scarborough. I am happy to report that in 2001 the Whitby Coat of Arms still hangs in the vestibule of the Harbour Office.

◆ ◆ ◆   ◆ ◆ ◆   ◆ ◆ ◆

From 1974 to 1978 the pleasure which I had enjoyed by working for Whitby Urban District Council had diminished under the pressure of Scarborough Borough Council and its attitude towards its smaller towns and villages, urban and rural.

For many years I had my name on a marine executive list and to my surprise one Boxing Day morning I received a call from Gray Mackenzie, a well known established port and marine company of the Middle East and Iranian Gulf.

'We think you are just the man we need in the Middle East,' were his opening words. 'Where in the Middle East?' I asked.

'Port of Jeddah, Saudi Arabia.'

I remembered that Jeddah was half way down the Red Sea and that when my ship was moving from Suez to Aden with the northerly wind behind us at the same speed as the ship, we had to turn round at least once each watch to get the vessel blown through. We conversed for a while but I said, 'I'm coming to London mid January,' so we made an appointment.

When I eventually saw Mr Mitchell he told me about the expansion of the port, numbers and sizes of ships – everything up to 100,000 ton tankers. I turned him down although his last words were: 'Can we contact you in about three or four months?'

'I can't see myself coming to Jeddah,' I said, 'but I'll leave it to you if you want to telephone me.'

Over the next few weeks Joyce and I would discuss from time to time our general life prospects under Scarborough Borough Council. We had been improving the Upper Harbour. Our idea was to dredge away the Bell shoal, the accumulation of many years of sludge washed down by the River Esk. Since Dr Beeching's fell hand in 1962, railway traffic to Whitby had been reduced to four trains per day and the odd wagon which would deliver coal to the once busy goods yard, now up for sale by British Rail.

My Deputy and I spent weeks planning how to improve the upper harbour and from time to time we met the Estates Surveyor of British Rail from York. We met as the Executive Committee of the Harbour, ie: The Chairman of the Harbour Committee of Whitby Urban District Council, his deputy councillor, my deputy and myself. On one hand we Harbour Masters were keen to buy the goods yard and reclaim the Bell shoal on to its top. Most of it could have worked, with a few dredgings out to sea.

But our councillors did not agree, and the British Rail Surveyor once said to me: 'Until you get another chairman, who might think your idea is all right. I'm not prepared to have another meeting.'

Today in Whitby we have a large supermarket and car parks where the goods yard used to stand. Our plan eventually was presented to the Harbour Committee who modified it. Although it was an opportunity for the mooring of over two hundred yachts in a beautiful harbour, my original idea to obtain a lovely water area from the bridge to Whitehall shipyard with a depth of five to seven feet did not materialise.

Just about this time there was a telephone call. 'There is a post again in Jeddah,' said Mr Mitchell. After some conversation I asked him how long I had to give him an answer. 'Give me a week,' I said, 'and thank you very much.' My own mind was to accept, but only if Joyce wanted to. We had a lot to think about. A week after the telephone interview it was 4 am when Joyce woke me and said: 'I've been thinking, and Jeddah is the place for us to go.'

♦ ♦ ♦   ♦ ♦ ♦   ♦ ♦ ♦

On 8th July 1978 I flew from Heathrow aboard a Lockhead Tristar and six hours later arrived at Jeddah airport in a temperature of ninety degrees. I had been sitting beside a young, talkative Arab girl who an hour before we landed disappeared into the toilet and half an hour later a lady dressed in black Arab robes and yashmak emerged and ignored my presence from then on.

We were transported by bus into the airport building where two queues were lined up. One for Saudi Arabians and one, much longer, for the rest of us. The Arab queue was cleared through the Immigration desks and into the Customs Hall and out into the city very quickly.

Our Immigration lot took a long time as well over a hundred passengers had come from the UK, like myself, to work for foreign companies doing work for the Saudi people. I had two suitcases full of personal things. I opened both cases and the Customs Officer asked me to take everything out to be seen. So then I had to re-pack it while he moved on to the next person. Then at the final gate all magazines and newspapers were scrutinised and any page three girls were confiscated.

I had been told by London that I would be met by someone in an electric blue suit and holding my name on a card displayed with many others. An Arab in a T shirt and jeans was calling out my name and one other. Hussein, the Arab, led us to a waiting car and we drove off through the very large city. We finally stopped in a side street with many impressive villas in its entire length of about a mile. 'Here's yours, Mr Stevenson,' he said, 'remember it's number 37 and you go to Town Office tomorrow.'

Before I had time to ask where it was and what taxi numbers were available he was off and I found myself in the hall of a big, boarding house type of villa. It was midnight and no one was around. All first floor rooms were occupied and I found a vacant one on the second floor and was pleased to get to bed, where I dropped off till 6.30 am. But all the rooms were now empty – I went through all three floors and all were vacant.

Downtown Jeddah, home to a million people. Small wonder that one of their major imports is cement.

In the basement was the catering group of people, an Australian firm who catered for the staff of Gray Mackenzie. One of these lads was most helpful. 'I'm going to Town Office and I can take you there. You have a lot of paper work to get through.' He was right. I was taken to the Personnel Officer, who greeted me warmly, then – took away my passport and gave me my Saudi ID card with my photograph on it. I also had to have a Port Pass to enter the port, a Ship Pass to board ships and a driving licence.

Next I was driven five miles up the Mecca Road to where Gray Mackenzie ran its vehicle centre. I was issued with car number 127. A Datsun 1200 which had been well used but had no air conditioning, which in our windy, hot city would have been a boon if you got lucky. I drove the car back to V37 with the manager's voice ringing in my ears. 'Never mind the traffic,' he said. 'If you prang with anybody, make sure he's not a Saudi, for if he is you'll be shipped off to the Police Station. And no one will know you're there till you miss your shift in port. All the best!' I managed to drive back to my 'home', but the way Saudi Arabs drove indicated no knowledge of a Highway Code.

The last instruction I had from Town Office was to drive 20 kms down town to Jeddah Islamic Port. Fortunately one of the fellows I met in the villa worked in the marine department and simply said: 'OK David, just follow me.' There were so many road works and coupled with my driving care I lost him. But I did find the road into the port, despite the volume of five line traffic, and was directed inside the gate where a seventy foot tall signal tower stood alongside No 2 Wharf with a huddle of office blocks around its foot.

A car pulled up and the British Harbour Master to whom I was introduced in his turn introduced me to the two other British pilots and the chief pilot over all, Mohammed Salamah and his three Saudi pilots, all of whom were his sons.

I was told by Mohammed to go with one of the British pilots who took me down the basin to No 10 berth where there lay quite a small ship with one tug attending. My colleague said: 'Can you do this one, David? I'll show you out of the inner gate and middle gate and we drop off into the cutter as we pass No 6 buoy.' My second ship that day was an American vessel of the 'Sealand' container company. This company had been keen on the early use of containers round the world. What they did was to buy up a lot of the wartime American T2 15,000 ton ships, put them in a dry dock, cut off the poop and turbine engine room, then insert a 100 foot section between bow and poop, increasing the length of the ship to 650 feet. Loaded with containers, this made an ungainly vessel which took a bit of skill to bring through the gates of Jeddah, down the basin and berth it on container berth No 16.

Facing page: Cement berth in full swing.

Ro Ro berth.

One of the things the British and temporary pilots had to do was to extract from the Admiralty chart of Jeddah and its reef-bound approach, go out in one of the pilot cutters and do their own marine survey of the areas, create anchorages and draw out copies of the areas for everyone. Within a few days I felt familiar with Jeddah port approaches, and by asking certain members of the Salamah and Ragaban families I learnt a lot.

One morning three weeks later the British Harbour Master caught up with me on No 2 Wharf to say, 'David, it is management's decision that from today you are the Senior British Pilot, making up duty rosters for all the pilots, – 15 British and 14 or so Saudi pilots.' Next day the chief pilot, Mohammed Salamah took me aside for a talk. 'David,' he said, 'I have been watching you, and we think you are a Scotch Arab.'

'Why do you say that?' I asked.

'Moslem and Christian are all one family,' he replied. 'We Moslems come from Ibrahim. It says so in Koran. It also says in Holy Bible that you come from Abraham and we are same-same.'

Nos 3, 4 & 5 out of a total of 25 berths.

He was seventy years old, a tall, angular but dignified figure. He told me he had been piloting ships from twenty miles off Jeddah since he was sixteen. His father, also Mohammed Salamah, took him off in the small family dhow. When a cable had been sent from Suez saying that a large ship was expected, Salamah would hoist that particular company's flag at the top of his mast and make a determined effort to reach the vessel before the other rival dhows.

The method of putting on board was to sail alongside the slow moving ship, catch on to a boat rope stretched alongside the vessel and a young, fit Arab would climb to the top of the lateen mast. The crew of the dhow would then

Unloading containers at No 23 berth.

sally their vessel from side to side, swinging the top mast to and fro till it touched the hull and the pilot could literally 'step' on board the ship. For this pilotage task the Captain would shake his hand and give him a small canvas bag in which were five sovereigns.

One day Salamah asked me to take him from the port to his house in the teeming centre of the city. Up four flights, greeted on each landing by an Arab lady, clad in the traditional black with yashmak, the whole atmosphere of the house having a welcoming air. I was taken into the family room, a large lounge with long settees all round the walls and comfortable chairs, to one of which I was escorted by a middle aged lady. All these women were Mohammed's wives, the youngest of whom carried in her arms a four-month old baby boy. Mohammed proudly took him up as he said with a broad smile: 'He is the future Chief Pilot of Jeddah. When he is sixteen I shall retire at the age of eighty-six.'

After some conversation, – some English but mostly Arabic – we left the family room and he took me into what he called his office. 'There is the money I made before King Khalid.' All along one wall were wooden tubs, once used as butter tubs, each one was closed by a cushion covered top. 'Take the cover off that one and you can sit on it afterwards,' he said. I removed the lid and my eyes were dazzled by the handfuls of gleaming sovereigns. What a surprise! When I sat down for the next hour of coffee and chat I just knew I should never again sit as 'richly.'

In 1976 all the shipping companies who were paid in gold had to pay dues to King Khalid and every Saudi pilot was paid a salary which was three times as much as the ex-pat pilots employed by Gray Mackenzie.

The only other family who were employed as pilots was that of Ali Ragaban and both families were well thought of in Jeddah and also the two other ports on the Red Sea. Yenbu and Gizan each about 200 miles north and south. Ali Ragaban was the old head of the Ragabans. At the age of sixty-five or so, he collapsed and died on a ship. We were all asked to attend his last farewells at 7 pm. The street in front of his house was cordoned off by the police and chairs were set out on both sides. Lots of family friends and those of us pilots, about twenty of us, queued at the corner of the street and formally greeted his sons, two of whom were pilots, then went and sat down for an hour or so. There were no ladies permitted to be in the street. The eldest son and Ali's widow came from the house and we were greeted by both and gave our condolences in Arabic, after which we dispersed and went home. Ali had died at 10 am. The last farewells were at 7 pm. But Ali had been rolled in a holy carpet and buried outside Jeddah in the desert in an unmarked grave.

There were about three dozen or so British port employees of Gray Mackenzie in villa No. 37 out of a total of about three hundred personnel. The port was organised by having a Port Operations Office, to which the marine and engineering branches reported. Forty-five berths had two men per berth, per ship. One looked after the large cargo shed, the other attended on the vessel alongside.

The average movements of shipping could be from sixty to a hundred ships in and out per twenty-four hours. With ships moving from 500 tons to 10,000 tons per vessel it certainly was a lot.

Each morning six pilots would be allocated movements. Two for vessels on berths, three to sea and one to Petromin tanker area to un-berth and to replace tanker traffic. So between six and ten o'clock there would be much marine

Pilots all: Keith Angus, Dave Stevenson, Norman Ross and Dave Booth.

traffic. Mornings took us off three or four miles to meet our ships in a fine humid day with the city of Jeddah fading into the morning mist. One of the things which showed up clearly from seaward was the large grain warehouse whose end, pointing out to sea and painted white, showed a very large Christian cross and made much comment in the shipping world. Within a few days the gable end of the warehouse was re-painted in three different dark colours.

I had been in the villa only a few days when a Scots lad who lived along the corridor invited me into his room and offered me a tot of whisky. 'Sorry, no,' I said. 'Our contract says at the end of it: – The only religion in Saudi Arabia is Islam. Alcohol is illegal.' He showed me his wardrobe, inside of which from floor to ceiling were the usual cardboard boxes which hold six bottles of whisky. I gasped at the thought of the police visiting our villa and arresting all of us for having so much whisky in the house.

'I've found out that you are a pilot,' Jock said. 'You and I can do business. All you have to do on container ships is to ask the Captain how much he has to sell and give him my name. You can be sure you'll have a good twenty per cent of what I get from the Saudis.' I was taken aback. 'What about our contract?' I asked. 'Alcohol is forbidden.'

He laughed. 'Who do you think ignores that rule? The Arabs themselves. Let me tell you this. I send all of my salary to my dear wife in Grangemouth. And this is what she is doing.' He took a photograph out of his hip pocket. It was of a fine modern bungalow. 'I'll do another year and then go home.' A week later he was in jail. The story eventually came out. His wardrobe was empty when a Saudi telephoned him and demanded six bottles of Scotch. 'I'm having a party,' he said. 'Tomorrow evening I need them.' That left Jock only a day to obtain the stuff. Being a ship stevedore, he asked a ship, just brought in, for some whisky and the Captain gave him two bottles. As he started to come down the gangway his opposite shed stevedore shouted 'Jock, they're on to you. Get rid of it – quick!' The coastguard policeman was cocking his pistol as Jock turned, ran to the offside of the ship and dropped the two bottles into the harbour. But when he came down, another coastguard truck was waiting for him. He was hand-cuffed, protesting, and carted off to the police station.

We residents of the villa were apprehensive for a day or two in case any of us might also be taken in. He was in jail for two and a half months, until Queen Elizabeth visited Riyadh and an amnesty was declared for lesser 'criminals'. We never saw Jock ever again.

◆ ◆ ◆   ◆ ◆ ◆   ◆ ◆ ◆

Another event which illustrates how careful an ex-pat has to be, living along-side the nationals of Saudi, happened to a young lad who was having his sleep continually disturbed by an adjacent household of young Saudis making an overnight concert of Arabic music. He was so roused one time that he went across to them and complained, picking up the offending tape recorder and went back home. That was about 4 am and by dawn two police cars arrived with one of the young Saudis who pointed out the offender and the tape re-corder. He was confined in the local prison, the Jeddah jail. His villa colleagues visited him every day with food, writing and toilet paper, soap etc. Visiting time was 6-8 pm, when dozens of visitors of all nationalities were herded together into the hall. It was divided into two rooms, each with a barred rail separated from each other by eight feet. Too far to hand anything to one's friend. The noise was infernal, for everyone tried to communicate with his friend at the top of his voice. The heat, the smell of prison and unwashed bodies were intolerable.

After three months work in the port I was due to get three weeks holiday. The day before I left, something most unusual occurred. Rain. Not the kind we are used to in Britain, but real monsoon type. As I drove home after work through the deluge under which hundreds of cars, buses and taxis all tried their best to stay on the road under which one to two feet of water just lay, awaiting sunshine and high temperature to dry off, for the carriageways had no gutters or drains. The five lanes had reduced to three and stop-start was the method of progress. I saw one car on the roof of which squatted the driver, waving his arms and shouting 'Yalla! Yalla! Help! Help!' but there was no one to help him. It rained off and on all night and I was woken by finding my bed, which stood against the outside wall, completely soaked as the rain drove right through the porous wall.

I was supposed to go to the airport that evening, but the flooding meant that all I could do was look out of my window at the slow moving river which covered the road. Twenty-four hours later I was able to get to the airport, landing in England six hours later and . . . home.

After a happy time with my family in Whitby I returned to Jeddah. In the vestibule of villa 37 were the personal effects of two of our friends, and the tale was this:

One of the boys was friendly with a young Saudi Airline hostess, originally from Cairo. They had met in London. One Friday, (the Islamic Sabbath) they together with a Gray Mackenzie friend, went off about thirty kilometres north of Jeddah to enjoy the lovely beaches and reefs. On the way back they had a flat tyre and as they were changing it one of the police cars which regularly patrol the Mecca Roads pulled up. The conversation was between the two Brits and the policeman and after 'Alykum salaam' they parted. A few miles further on they were unlucky enough to have another puncture. Alas! No spare tyre. While they were pondering what to do, the same patrol car pulled up. This time they spoke to the air hostess. She replied, not in English but in Egyptian Arabic, not the same as that spoken in Jeddah. This made the police suspicious and despite their protests the three were taken off to the nearest police station.

Both men were charged with sexual assault and she was charged with illegal sex with two foreigners. We heard no more for a while. Months later a pick-up truck arrived at the Operations Office manned by four policemen and handed the two men, handcuffed and shackled, into the care of the company. Both boys looked very careworn and thin after their time in prison. They were flown out that evening, but it was weeks before their luggage left our villa. We did hear later that the girl was helped by her Saudi Air colleagues to switch with a friend and land in London as a proper air hostess.

To the north of Jeddah the beaches and reefs were a wonderful world. A family of two young marrieds and their children would join my wife and I and we would drive about twenty miles up the Mecca Road, then we turned off the road and drove due west in clouds of sand and dust. James, the young father, led the way and we pulled up 300 yards from the gleaming sea. We carried our picnic things and large umbrellas over to the beach. The sun broiled us alive, but under the shade of the brollies and sun-protection cream we could play on the beach and go out to the edge of the reef, a quarter of a mile out to sea. One walked waist-high through azure water like silk to ones skin, pausing to watch the tiny humbug fish which dashed into a coral nodule as one passed. The children loved this, running and swimming in the gradually deepening water on top of the reef down to some ten feet before it shallowed up to the edge of the reef where the waves of the Red Sea broke in a creamy flurry of small waves. We had brought our snorkel masks and stood on the precipitous edge and launched off to face downwards, gazing at the vertical coral cliff, disappearing slowly into an ever increasing indigo blue. From the dozens of coral clefts could be seen the gaping mouth of the multi-coloured grouper, the snake-like head of the Moray Eel, while all around was the glory of hundreds of fish of all colours. It was a world of paradise. At one time the eldest girl, Rebecca, was splashing ahead of us. Suddenly, there was a great flurry of splashing. We feared it was a shark, but it was an eight foot wide Manta Ray which shot over the reef edge. For the rest of that day we kept a good lookout for sharks. There were big sharks off Jeddah, but what had happened in the port had come about due to the tremendous increase in the imports of livestock. For many years sheep, goats and camels were brought over the Red Sea in a trip of about twenty-four hours. Small 1500 ton coastal ships would bring two or three thousand sheep and goats, camels too, but they were just for meat. Other fine young dromedaries were brought in a small, special ship to be bought by wealthy Saudis and used for racing, rather like our horse races. They were ridden by small boy jockeys and the Saudi owners would bet with one another.

In a bit of bad weather a small livestock ship loaded with about three thousand sheep and goats was driven on to the reef some five miles south of Jeddah. Complications arose. We had no such lifeboat arrangements in Jeddah, so the crew were saved by friends. But, alas, what of the animals? One of Gray Mack's men who looked after the livestock quays kept an eye on them by visiting the reef one or twice a week and reporting to Port Operations. But nothing was done by Arab buyers and sellers, and those poor beasts were allowed to perish in dreadful thirst and shocking heat.

Around 1982 the importing of Merino sheep from Adelaide, South Australia, became frequent. One morning I was sent out to bring in a 90,000 livestock ship called *Polaris*. Previously these ships were usually converted old tankers, easily recognised by the decks of livestock pens. I got out to four miles and all I could see was a beautiful, white Cunard Line ship about seven miles away. I kept asking the control tower, 'I'm out here looking for *Polaris* and all I can see is a recognisable Cunarder.' Back came the answer: 'What you are looking at is *Polaris*.'

We approached her and as we swung to go alongside a great wave of animal smell overwhelmed us, and as I walked up from the pilot ladder to the bridge, each pen which held eight sheep had water and food pellets for the animals.

The ship was officered and manned by Norwegian people and flew the ensign of Panama. I discovered that she had been a Cunard liner which caught fire a few miles from Port Everglades to which she had been bound. The efficiency and skill of the captain and crew meant that all passengers were saved, but the ship became a 'constructive total loss,' *ie* far too expensive to be re-furbished and most likely to be scrapped.

From 1982 to 1985, when I left Jeddah, the volume of livestock traffic from South Australia steadily increased. The voyage trans-ocean took 3-4 weeks and the number of sheep lost was quite high. Quite a lot of carcases were dropped in the Red Sea approach to Jeddah, consequently the number of sharks increased and we had to be very careful if we went swimming close to the port.

Livestock carrier from Fremantle with 30,000 head of lamb.
One could smell them for three miles downwind.

In early 1985 the contract of the company was due for renewal. In competition with companies of the world, particularly Philippines and Korea, both of whom reduced their charges from ours by at least a half. So what we were offered in our new contract meant no private car, no wives in good accommodation, sharing not only transport but going back to bachelor style housing, and leave reduced from twenty-one days to eighteen days every three months. We did not re-sign and came home to settle in our favourite home town the ancient but good port to be in –

'For Whitby binds us to herself –
We folk who love her well.'

APPENDIX I

Tom Bink's Alternative History of the Port of Whitby

The following events happened a long time ago. Most of the people and events are past history but I feel I should record them as I remember them, before my memory and recollection goes completely.

I have been told, though I've never read it, nor seen it in print that around 1880/90 the North Eastern Railway Company as it then was, approached the Harbour Trustees and suggested a plan. The railway company would dredge out the harbour and build a deep water quay right alongside the Railway Station, entirely at Company expense, with the object of developing Whitby as a steam trawler port. This suggestion was turned down flat because Whitby thought such a development would not be in keeping with its new found status as a holiday resort. Whether true or false, and should it true, this story illustrates the conflict between those whose purpose was to develop the town still further as a resort, and those who wanted to develop in a way to provide jobs for the fishermen and sailormen of Whitby, something the holiday/tourist trade does not generally do.

During the years of the Second World War Whitby was practically dead as a harbour. If not quite moribund it clung to life with all the vigor of a damp squib. The piers were blocked off with barbed wire for security reasons. There were no navigation lights on the lighthouses, and a part time watchman, titled grandly Harbour Master, kept an eye on the port.

There was by 1948 a Customs and Excise Officer, one Tom Binks who had several other manifestations of his job. Receiver of Wrecks, Superintendent of Mercantile Marine, Registrar of Royal Naval Reserve. In fact any marine aspects of Her Majesty's Government so far as Whitby Port and Harbour was concerned, came under Tom's office.

A Harbour Master had been appointed by the Whitby Urban District Council, who, sometime in the twenties had acquired the Trusteeship of the Port and Harbour of Whitby Strand. In 1948, the whole area of the harbour had a general air of neglect and decay. The small keel boats of the small fishing fleet (Galilee, Endeavour, Easter Morn, Success) would have to lie outside the piers to wait the rising tide to give enough water to get over the Bar and so to the ancient Fish Quay. Some forty or so yachts and small craft belonging to Whitby

Yacht Club, brought a touch of glamour in the summer months. The dredger 'Esk,' built in 1936, was comparatively new but was seldom seen at work. This was because Whitby Urban District Council hadn't the money to spare for dredging because there was little or no *income* from the harbour. *Esk* would lay up on the mud of the Bell Shoal in the Upper Harbour during the winter months. In spring a brief charter to other local ports would bring in enough revenue to finance a few months dredging mostly on the Bar and lower channel and that was not nearly enough to cope with the constant deposits of river mud and the sand brought in by the winter gales.

The old wooden Fish Quay was rotten, and so were the even more ancient stone wharves along the Upper Church Street on the East Side. On the West Side alongside the railway sidings, between Dock End and Bog Hall were grassy banks from which protruded occasional stone remains of interest only to historians and archaeologists. To complete the picture the main piers and extensions had been neglected for so long that wave action had carved out great caverns in them. There was about the place a strange atmosphere of complacency and fatalism. The local fishermen had had the harbour to themselves for so long that to all intents and purposes it was theirs alone, and perhaps they wanted it to stay that way. A sentiment had grown up that Whitby was unsuitable for ordinary shipping. This hardly stood up to the previous history of Whitby, which had at one time been the sixth port in England. Whitby was still classed as a 'harbour of refuge' and for that reason tolls had been levied on passing ships by London Trinity House. This general feeling of hopelessness was widespread. Indeed many years later, a visiting importing ships master mentioned that while he had anchored waiting for a pilot to come, a passing ship had signalled to him. 'What are you doing there? There's nothing for you in that place.'

The Harbour Master of the day, one Captain Hardy would quite openly state that whenever he got an enquiry from an owner or agent he would reply that Whitby had no facilities for loading or unloading ships. Regrettably he was speaking the truth.

So here it was. Whitby – a fine old port on the brink of collapse. The one redeeming feature was the annual herring season when for six weeks in July to September about 100 Scots herring boats would land herring every day and bring the harbour to life for that brief period. At the same time Dutch and German fishing boats would call for brief periods and their crews would lend colour and pleasure to the busy harbour scene. Alas, always too brief. To watch an entire fishing fleet departing for the fishing grounds on a summer evening was a memorable sight and one of the highlights of summer.

Three wholly unconnected events began the rejuvenation of the Port. Unconnected and unforeseen strokes of fortune. A very severe storm – a change of Harbour Master, and a dock strike in Hull. On 31st January 1953 a northerly gale of Hurricane force combined with High Spring Tides to produce a SEICHE or storm surge. Right into the North Sea. Holland was inundated, parts of the East Coast of England were flooded, including Canvey Island on the Thames. In the Irish Sea the ferry Princess Victoria was overwhelmed and sank with tragic loss of life.

Many will remember the great storm of 1978 when immense numbers of trees were uprooted, houses damaged but fortunately no one was killed. The media, who apparently all lived in the South, proclaimed it the worst storm for 100 years. It was not. In Whitby the area around Dock End was awash and the yards leading from New Quay Road to Baxtergate were flooded. Upper Church Street was also under water for a time.

Something like 300 British people died in the 1953 storm and many more in Holland. It was a great disaster but it led almost directly to the renaissance of Whitby, for the old wooden Fish Quay was damaged beyond repair.

It just so happened that the Government of the day, concerned with nuclear strikes on major ports and cities developed the policy of building deep water quays in such small ports as were suitable so that the seaborne trade could be continued. Whitby's need for a new Fish Quay came exactly at the right time to qualify for assistance, and so the fine modern 700 feet of Fish Quay replaced the old rickety structure. This was the first stroke of luck.

The second was that Captain Hardy took himself off to Ramsgate in Kent. How he got on with his new superiors was never discovered as he never returned to Whitby. His replacement was a very different sort of man, Captain Frank Graves. Not an easy man to get on with, as various members of the Council were to discover. By some people he was actively disliked, but he did want one thing. He could foresee that Whitby Port had a future, to be a trading port. There was a lot of short sea and coastal traffic on the go at this time in the fifties and Whitby was in a good position geographically to Scandinavian and Low Country ports. Also around this time Whitehall Shipyard under the ownership of Whitby Shipbuilding and Engineering Company, had started to build modern seine net fishing vessels for the Grimsby fleet. So there was the beginning of a revival in the Fishing Industry.

The third stroke of luck was a dock strike one fine day in June in the great port of Hull. A great shipment of potatoes had built up in continental ports for England and the owners were desperate to get them moving. A phone call from Thos E Kettlewell of Goole, to Captain Graves asked. 'Could you handle some shiploads of potatoes into Whitby?' Hardy would have given a resounding 'NO'. Graves reply was. 'Send as many as you like. We'll handle them.'

Now this was when the new Fish Quay was not yet finished and virtually unusable. Nevertheless, a few days later three small cargo ships arrived on the same tide, laden with sacks of potatoes. Graves put one alongside St Ann's Staith, one on New Quay Road and one in Dock End basin. Full employment then was the order of the day, so the best the Employment Exchange could do was to scrape together all the unemployables, ne'er do wells, and outright pirates to form a labour force. A local haulage contractor produced lorries. Tom Binks concluded paper formalities at the Custom House, and the unloading began, under the able direction of Captain Gordon Cook the Dredger Master, also a Master Mariner. The ships' derricks operated manually swung to and fro while crowds of fascinated holiday makers gazed at the free spectacle. Most of them had probably never seen a ship before at close quarters. In a couple of days the ships sailed outwards in ballast and the following week three more ships arrived.

But this time there was a difference. The unemployables had discovered by chatting in the pubs that they were now '*dockers*' and as such they went on strike for more pay. This they did. Work stopped and the future of the Harbour hung in balance. Not for long. Graves was an astute man. He spread the word on the Fish Quay that the dockers two day's pay was more than a fisherman would get for seven day's fishing. The fishermen lined up at the Harbour Office to sign on for the dock work and finished the unloading job. Whitby's reputation was saved and Ketlewell's never thereafter lost faith in the port.

Now you might, in your innocence have thought that Captain Graves and his staff might have received some credit for doing such a difficult job successfully. You would be wrong. There was never a chance of any congratulations or thanks. According to reports which emanated at the time the Council's reaction was something on the lines of. 'What right had the Harbour Master, without consulting them – to risk damaging the roadways and footpaths right at the start of the holiday season, let alone cluttering up the town's harbourside where people walked, with filthy, dusty bags of potatoes and lorries.'

These same worthy councilors, the butchers, bakers, candlestick makers were the very people who constantly made speeches, extolling the past glories of 'this ancient and historic seaport'. Yet they were quite unaware that the very harbourside roads and pavements from Victoria Steps (Opposite the Cutty Sark Pub) northwards to and including Scotch Head were designated 'the Legal Quays of Whitby as a Customs Port'. These Legal Quays included part of Dock End Car Park, Victoria Steps which had been filled in from the harbour by the Council in 1936 – probably illegally if put to the test; and New Quay Road, St Ann's Staith, Marine Parade and the Fish Quay. All were authorized places for the landing and shipping of goods – *All* goods. The mind boggles at the thought of bulk crude oil coming ashore at Marine Parade!

The fact remained that the potato ships had been handled at proper legal quays. The Council was flabbergasted by this revelation, but had to accept the situation. This of course put Graves in the right but did not increase his popularity in certain quarters of the Council, particularly as he was not slow to point out his position as Harbour Master under the Harbour Acts and Orders.

This ill will seems to have festered on for several years till it led to his dismissal some years later. The Treasurer was somewhat mollified when he saw revenue begin to come in from the ships in the form of Dues and Wharfage on the goods. The Council had been very slow to realize that money could be made in this way and the *Scale of Harbour Dues and Charges* had not been revised for many decades.

The next stage in harbour development came a year or two later. There was a deficiency of limestone in farmlands in parts of Scotland. Just the type of limestone tailings which come from the quarries of Arthur Slater of Pickering and Thornton le Dale. The Government introduced a subsidy on lime if it was delivered to Scotland. Slater wanted to ship limestone but discovering that some of the destinations were islands (Orkney & Shetland), found ships would be cheaper than road transport. He first tried Scarborough who turned him down flat. But when he approached the Whitby Harbour Master and suggested that if a trial shipment was successful it would be followed by a hundred more. This was just the kind of regular trade Captain Graves was waiting for and he grabbed the opportunity.

Of course, you would be right in guessing that all would not go smoothly. Murphy's Law decreed that the holiday season was in full swing. The new Fish Quay was complete, more than long enough for the fishing fleet. Graves used the North End of the quay, near Scotch Head, to berth the 300-500 ton ships. The actual loading of the ship was not too easy. Fleets of lorries loaded with limestone tailings rolled up and discharged their loads through a chute, directly into the ships' hold. This they would do only one at a time, which led to congestion along Pier Road, plus a certain amount of dust, which on Whitbys' windy quayside, soon raised howls of protest from the adjoining shops and businesses. There were also voices complaining of blocking the fine new promenade which the Fish Quay had become.

Very soon Slater had a big new storage shed through which the receiving and loading of lime was done with improved methods of loading. There were still protests about the disfiguring of a promenade with an ugly shed – never mind that the quay was a *Legal Quay* etc and the ships held a fascination for tourists. Mr Sam Deeks who owned the Amusement arcade directly opposite the lime shed and who might have been expected to be the loudest complainant was heard to say on more than one occasion that the presence of the shed actually helped his business. People walking along the Fish Quay (promenade) when faced with the big shed, automatically crossed the road, right into Sam's Arcade. He was a happy man.

In the upper harbour above the Swing Bridge shipping activity had begun to stir. The local firm of timber merchants Corner and Brown, who in pre-war days had shipped one barge per annum of timber from the Baltic, were taken over by a nationwide company called Williams-Evans who begun to bring frequent if not regular timber imports to Whitby into Dock End Basin.

Despite Captain Graves constant efforts to attract more trade, he was handicapped by a genuine lack of facilities. Neither the Fish Quay nor Dock End as it then was, were ideal for working cargos. There were no shore cranes or handling gear and it was a slow and expensive business using ships' gear. The dredging had improved as money had begun to come in from Fish and Harbour Dues but the harbour was still badly silted up south of Dock End to Bog Hall.

The Council had come round to the view that shipping trade was a good thing, to be encouraged. Some of them prompted by Graves and a few more like minded people came to the idea that more berthage was needed if the trade was to expand.

Kettlewell's had established a presence in Whitby and they had an office in Pier House, the old Harbour Office. They undertook the agency and ship-broking business as it grew. Around this time the Normanby Report was commissioned on the future prospects of the town and harbour of Whitby and Professor Daysh, of Durham University visited Whitby, called on the Customs Officer and Captain Graves to check on the numbers of fishing vessels and marine craft using the port. Tom Binks pushed the idea to the Professor of a new wharf alongside the Railway Station and no doubt Captain Graves would add his ideas on how valuable a railhead alongside a dock could be to a small port. Very few small ports had such a feature. When the report came out it stated that just such a wharf would be the right way forward. Here was the goal to aim for. However, the Mills of God grind slowly and it was a further six to eight years before a wharf came into being, continuous to and at right angles to Dock End Basin. The original suggestion was for only 100 feet of wharf, but Councillor Richard Wastell, who had more vision, moved for 200 feet, and so Endeavour Wharf came into being. The Council did a good job; they paid £5,000 to British Rail to have a siding laid on to the wharf. So all the portents were good. Business was moving, ships were coming; more fishing boats were being bought and built in Scotland at Millers' Yard St Monance, and being added to the local fleet. More yachtsmen had found Whitby to be an accommodating and welcoming haven. All this meant increased harbour revenue. Then disaster. A gentleman called Dr Beeching started to axe British Railways' so called uneconomic lines. Mr Peasegood, Kettlewell's General Manager in Goole went to the BR people in York prepared to guarantee a million pounds worth of business per annum if the Whitby/Malton link to York was retained. Now, had the wharf been completed a year or two earlier so that the regular movement of freight from Whitby/York had been established the result might have been different. But it was too late, and the following years have been a testimony to lack of foresight and determination. The hundreds of heavily laden articulated lorries, carrying steel, chemicals, timber and timber products bound to manufacturers in the West Riding and Midlands have ground their way endlessly up Prospect Hill, through Sleights, up Blue Bank and over the moors in all weathers. To the frustration and danger to other road users. We all know the folly, nationwide, of driving so much rail freight on to the roads.

Dr Beeching was rewarded for his efforts with a peerage and a seat in the House of Lords.

In 1964, Frank Graves' reward for foresight and tremendous efforts to promote Whitby Harbour as a viable port, was quite different. In one of his many 'exchanges of view' with a councilor, he was held to have been rude. There may have been other reasons which never were disclosed. But the end result for him was a vote of no confidence and – dismissal.

APPENDIX II

The ship yard that was murdered –

*The story of the Whitby Ship Building and Engineering Co Ltd
as told by Tom Binks.*

Those of you, who are familiar with the history of the 1920's and 30's will remember the story of Jarrow on Tyne which became known as the 'Town that was murdered' when Palmers Shipyard & Steelworks, on which most of the town depended for employment closed down as 'surplus to requirements'. You will recall that Palmers the owners of the yard, were the builders of what is now Grinkle Park Hotel, and also Port Mulgrave from which hundreds of tons of iron ore were shipped up the coast to the yard at Jarrow each year.

What I am about to tell you is not the murder of a town, but strangely enough, of a shipyard, while the town looked on unable to help. This is a topic which has become all too familiar these days, with the difference that it is about a small yard that could, and should have survived. The shipyard is the one that became such a burden to the Borough of Scarborough that they sold it as a sewerage works site. An end more degrading than that can hardly be imagined. But it was not they who killed the yard. The foul deed of murder was done many years before Scarborough had the power to inflict humiliation on one of Whitby's historic sites.

The subject of my tale is the rise and disastrous fall of a gallant attempt to revive one of Whitby's traditional industries; the building of wooden ships, small ones it is true, but none the worse for that.

The Whitby Shipbuilding & Engineering Co Ltd, was the brainchild of two enterprising and talented men. One of them, always referred to as 'Billy' Eves, who was the proprietor of the motor business which still carries his name. He was, I believe the driving force behind the shipyard. The other partner was Marcus Fletcher, the technical expert, works manager and designer, who was an experienced and talented wooden shipbuilder.

It was in the wake of the Second World War that these two men formed a company and acquired the long derelict Whitehall Shipyard where the Turnbull family had once built iron steamships. Some of the old buildings were still in place and formed the nucleus of the new company's workshops and stores.

The market that Eves and Fletcher were after was less ambitious than the Turnbulls had catered for, but was more practical for modern times *ie* the

Danish type of seine net fishing boat of which the *Helga Maria* was a notable example before her conversion to private use. Why this? You may ask.

It all goes back to wartime days when large numbers of Danish skippers with their boats and crews fled across the North Sea, and settled in Grimsby. The boats were highly efficient by the standards of the time, and had small crews of just three or four men. When the war ended many of them continued to fish out of Grimsby and of course in those halcyon days of the North Sea teeming with fish, they did very well. During the late forties and fifties there were said to be several hundred Danish seine netters at Grimsby, and sooner or later they would need replacing with new vessels. This was the market that Eves and Fletcher saw as an opportunity to establish Whitby as leading centre for building replacement vessels.

One of the yard's first jobs however, was not a fishing boat at all, but the conversion of an old RNLI pulling lifeboat into a cabin cruiser named *Janderval*. The woodwork for this vessel was constructed by an old timer who had learned his trade in Turnbull's yard in the early 1900's, so there was a small degree of continuity with the craftsmanship of the past. The owner of *Janderval* took her off to Holland for a holiday. On the return journey he ran into really foul weather, and was so sea-sick that he never took *Janderval* to sea again.

For the real start to the yard, Mark Fletcher designed a fifty ton boat with sea-keeping qualities that would enable it to fish in Icelandic and North Atlantic waters for up to three weeks at a time. It would be equipped with a full suit of sails for use while fishing. They were made in the sail loft of the old shipyard. Meanwhile Billy Eves was spending a lot of his time talking to Danish skippers in Grimsby, and managed to get orders for a couple of boats which in due course were built in Whitby.

Just as business was beginning to warm up. Iceland threw a spanner in the works by extending her territorial waters to fifty miles, which was the start of the first of the 'cod wars', culminating when Iceland extended her waters to 200 miles a decade or so ago, when the second 'cod war' tactics by the Icelandic Coastguard Cutters was to cut the nets of the British trawlers inside the 200 mile limit. The Royal Navy frigates used in a fishery protection role were not as manoeuvrable as the smaller Icelandic cutters, which literally sailed rings around them. This removed at a stroke some of Britain's best fishing grounds, and indeed within a few years led to the demise of the British distant water fishing fleet; indeed the Fish Dock at Hull has been filled in and is now a supermarket and car park, the remainder of it small industrial units.

Not to be outdone Marcus Fletcher designed a smaller boat of thirty-five tons, more suited to home waters. Of the original fifty ton boats, one demonstrated its seaworthiness by re-registering in the Bahamas, and another in one of the West African ports.

By the time I arrived in Whitby in 1948, the company from a standing start had worked up to an output of about two vessels per annum. By careful management they had built up a reserve of capital, and by judicious second hand purchase had created a machine shop which enabled them to undertake all necessary engineering work.

At the same time they were training men as shipwrights. There were also evening institute classes for apprentices (and anyone else) in the craft of boat-building. By the middle of the 1950's the company had broken into the local market by building a couple of keelboats for local owners, thus breaking the virtual monopoly of Scottish boat-builders.

Among the projects Marcus Fletcher had lined up for the future, was to build a replica of Cook's *Endeavour* here in his own Whitby yard. There is no doubt he could have done it, and at a fraction of the cost of later estimates. This is proved by the small replica *Endeavour* now hanging in the main hall of the Cleveland Centre in Middlesbrough which was built here in Whitby Shipyard by Hugh Gollogly one time boat builder with Marcus Fletcher. It should be realised that the eighteenth century builders did not usually work from plans; there were no plans in existence from which a replica could be built. So Marcus drew up a set of plans for his own future use. In the confusion of the subsequent sale of the yard these plans were thought to have been lost. Eventually according to news-paper reports, the missing plans turned up in Australia of all places and were used in building the Western Australia replica recently completed.

At this time the future of the yard looked reasonably secure. What went wrong?

What the company had in mind was not so much the building of new vessels as the refitting of the existing fleet of seiners. To equip the yard adequately for dealing with the stream of boats they foresaw, they had to have a slipway to draw the boats up out of the water. At this point I must admit I never under-stood why the old slipway used in the Turnbull days could not have been repaired and adapted, or reconstructed sufficiently to deal with small fishing boats. The owners of the yard must have considered this possibility, and the fact is that rightly or wrongly they rejected it in favour of a new slip. This would cost more than the company could raise from its own resources, but at the time there was in being a Government grant and loan scheme administered by the Board of Trade, and designed to help small businesses to expand.

This could be a godsend to the company, and too good for them to miss. They applied to the Board of Trade, submitted plans for the proposed new slipway which were accepted as reasonable, and work began. At first all went well, but before long the contractors ran into trouble, and from that point noth-ing ever again went right for the company. From a layman's point of view I can best describe the problem as the unsuspected equivalent of a quicksand in the bed of the river which sent the cost of the operation up in the region of £60,000 which was more than the company could raise even with the Government grant. £60,000 may not sound very much in our debased currency, but this was thirty years ago. The modern equivalent would be in the order of £2 - £3 million .

Most people in Whitby will tell you it was the cost of the slipway that broke the company's back, but there was much more to it than that. The Board of Trade was prepared to help out with a loan on condition that the Whitby company took on board a financial adviser nominated by the Department. This was not as unreasonable you may think, as a safeguard against the misuse of public money. Yet Eves and Fletcher between them had built up a business literally from nothing, and managed it successfully for some fifteen years. They had no choice; it was either accept the offer or go bust.

So now the financial advisor comes on the scene. You will hardly believe the rest of the sad tale, but it is absolutely true. It was in the course of conversation with one or other of the two men deeply concerned that I heard about the progress of events as they were happening. It was not told me in confidence, or in the course of my official business. Both men felt so strongly about it that they must have talked to others. They have both been dead for so many years that I see no reason for not passing on to you what they told me so freely, and in so doing clear their names of the charge of bankrupting their own business.

The 'Financial Adviser' nominated by the Board of Trade turned out to be the boss of a business in Middlesbrough well known in its field, but with no connection whatever with ship or boatbuilding. Perhaps that was seen as an advantage. Whether or not that was the case the reason for his selection by the Board of Trade remains a mystery. I shall refer to him only as Mr X for his arrival was the fatal blow that caused the life-blood of the company to drain away. Mr X made the condition that he would accept the job of financial adviser only if he were made Managing Director of the company. This came as a bitter blow to our two worthies, because as you can imagine the last thing they needed was to have to hand over control of their business to a stranger. The only alternative open to them was to forego the financial help from the Government; this they were in no position to do. They appealed to the Board of Trade to find them an alternative adviser, but it was to no avail and very unwillingly they gave in.

So that is how and why Mr X became Managing Director of the Whitby Shipbuilding & Engineering Co Ltd.

Presently he announced his plan for the future of the yard. Remember this was a yard designed, equipped and staffed for the building of wooden craft, and there was a potential market ready to hand.

Mr X announced he was going to build steel barges. Where he got this notion from and why he thought he could do it I have no idea. What is certain is he didn't get a single order. From the day he was appointed the company's output was nil, and the business was doomed.

I have seen Marcus Fletcher scarlet with rage while the yard that was his pride and joy was being destroyed, and he could do nothing about it. One summer day Billy Eves, in an obvious state of deep depression, said to me that if that man (Mr X) went on as he was doing the yard would be bankrupt by Christmas, and it was.

The customary Xmas Dinner for the employees was held at Bothams old cafe in Baxtergate, (now occupied by Boots) and the following day or shortly after they were told they were all sacked because the company was bankrupt.

Thus by taking control of the company out of the hands of the people who created it, the so called financial adviser killed it. Can the destruction of this promising company be described otherwise than as wilful murder? Our legal friends may object that this is all hearsay; there is no evidence. To that I would reply that this is not a prosecution; it is history.

Mr X's motive for taking on a job that events proved he was incapable of doing remains a mystery. You may think that a responsible Government department like the Board of Trade would not allow such a thing to happen, but the fact remains – they did, though probably with the best of intentions. Theirs was the responsibility for selecting the 'financial adviser' and compelling the company to accept him.

Captain Bill Pickering, sought help from them in connection with the construction of his Riverside Wharf in Church Street (Pickerings Wharf). He discussed the shipyard case with them (to make sure the same thing did not happen to him) and they admitted (he said), that they had made one 'hell of a bloomer'. And in his own words 'there were many red faces at the Board of Trade'.

The yard was put up for sale, and it was bought for a nominal sum. The figure of £15,000 lingers in my mind, but it may be wrong. It was still a fully equipped shipyard with a brand new unused slipway. It might even then have been salvaged had it been bought by someone who shared the hopes and aspirations of its founders, and was able to inject some capital into it.

In the event it became the property of a man, who if I may borrow a Yorkshire phrase was (in my opinion) 'nobbut a wealthy playboy' who had no more interest in building fishing boats than had Mr X, and to whom the shipyard was just his latest toy, to be played with for a time and then discarded. He converted the old sail loft into what he called 'The Shipyard Club' and decorated the walls with what had been Marcus Fletcher's working drawings.

The experts tell us that nobody dies of a broken heart, but my guess is that if anybody ever did it was those two men, Billy Eves and Marcus Fletcher. They deserved a better fate. Whitby too would have been a better place had not their plans been fatally sabotaged.